Praise for *The Misleading Mind*

"Readers of *The Misleading Mind* are in for a special treat. Not only has Karuna Cayton recast the profound psychological insights of the traditional Buddhist teachings in accessible, contemporaneous language, he has illustrated these transformative insights vividly by drawing upon case histories of those he has counseled in his psychotherapeutic practice. His presentation is further enriched by the intimate glimpse it gives of two inspiring masters — Lamas Thubten Yeshe and Zopa Rinpoche — who embody the compassion, wisdom, and humor that are the hallmark of true mental health."

— Jonathan Landaw, teacher and author of
Buddhism for Dummies and *Images of Enlightenment*

"Karuna Cayton has had the very great fortune to be a heart-disciple of two remarkable and irreplaceable Tibetan Lamas. This book distills the essential practices of Mahayana mind-transformation that Karuna has received, cultivated, and taught over many decades. *The Misleading Mind* shares the profound depth of Buddhist psychological wisdom in a wonderfully inviting and accessible way. I highly recommend it."

— Peter Fenner, PhD, teacher and author of *Radiant Mind*

"*The Misleading Mind* is not another book on how to overcome the challenges of life. It is much more than that. It offers time-tested and practical tools for realizing our incredible potential and working toward becoming fulfilled and happy beings. Karuna Cayton has been immersed in Eastern thought for decades and communicates its psychology and methods in an easy, understandable, and yet profound way. This is truly a manual for becoming a happier and kinder person."

— Rasmus Hougaard, managing director of the Potential Project

"Through his many years of deep study of Buddhist psychology, sincere introspection, and work at helping others, Karuna Cayton has gained genuine wisdom, which he generously shares in *The Misleading Mind*. Skillfully integrating ancient wisdom with everyday stories of home and work life, Karuna reveals very practical methods for working with your own mind to discover greater satisfaction and joy in your real life. Like the skilled therapist and wise parent that he is, Karuna doesn't promise quick fixes; rather he provides genuine insights and methods that with sustained effort will bring about meaningful changes. This is a clear, grounded, and useful guidebook for working with the mind and heart."

— Lorne Ladner, PhD, psychologist and author of
The Lost Art of Compassion

"*The Misleading Mind* is a self-help manual full of accurate descriptions of traditional Buddhist teachings, recipes for mental health, and a map of the paths leading to a productive and well-balanced life. This wise and thoughtful book will help beginners who know little or nothing about Buddhism take responsibility for their own happiness. Seasoned practitioners of meditation will also find commonsense advice for training and transforming the mind."

— Jeffrey Hopkins, professor emeritus at the University of
Virginia and president of the UMA Institute for Tibetan Studies

"Karuna Cayton's analysis and method in *The Misleading Mind* are well thought-out and should be a great help to readers. It will help them truly understand what the Buddha said: 'You are your own guide and your own enemy. It depends on how you use your mind.' From this understanding, you can liberate numberless sentient beings. This is the true potential of the mind."

— Lama Zopa Rinpoche, spiritual director of the
Foundation for the Preservation of the Mahayana Tradition

THE
MISLEADING
MIND

THE
MISLEADING
MIND

HOW WE CREATE OUR
OWN PROBLEMS AND HOW
BUDDHIST PSYCHOLOGY
CAN HELP US SOLVE THEM

Karuna Cayton

New World Library
Novato, California

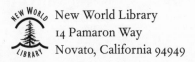

New World Library
14 Pamaron Way
Novato, California 94949

Text design and typography by Tona Pearce Myers

Library of Congress Cataloging-in-Publication Data
Cayton, Karuna, date.
 The misleading mind : how we create our own problems and how Buddhist psychology can help us solve them / Karuna Cayton.
    p.   cm.
 ISBN 978-1-57731-942-9 (pbk. : alk. paper)
 1. Buddhism—Psychology. I. Title.
 BQ4570.P76C39 2012
 294.3'444—dc23   2011048858

First printing, March 2012
ISBN 978-1-57731-942-9
Printed in the USA on 100% postconsumer-waste recycled paper

  New World Library is a proud member of the Green Press Initiative.

10 9 8 7 6 5 4

This book is dedicated to you, the reader.
Without a reader, there is no book.
And without a book, there is no author.
May all your troubles dissolve into space.

Contents

Introduction

To everyone who has ever gone to a therapist, bought a self-help book, consulted an astrological chart, or cracked open a fortune cookie in hopes of finding the answer or key to lasting happiness, *The Misleading Mind* offers a radical message. There is no key. There is no single answer that can be wrapped in a cookie. However, we can achieve lasting emotional health and happiness if we learn to train our minds. We each have the potential to alleviate our own suffering and embody our most wonderful, authentic self in each and every moment, but only if we learn to master the nasty tricks that our mind — by its very nature — plays on us. To put it another way, this book is written with the belief that every one of us has the potential to become an Olympic athlete in our mental development, but only if we train with the requisite intensity and drive.

The Misleading Mind offers a powerful approach to our mental health. It takes the basic tenets of Buddhist psychology and methodically explores the nature of our problems and how they take root in our lives. Then, by training ourselves in the use of simple yet effective mental practices, we can gradually learn to identify the unhelpful thought patterns that contribute to our problems and solve them in the moment. We can, in a way, become our own therapists and spiritual guides: learning to study and understand our problems on our own, taking firm ownership over them and transforming them, and, ultimately, translating our new awareness into action in the world.

In Buddhism, suffering is considered both a universal and a subjective state. Everyone suffers, and the causes of suffering are always internal. Modern psychology also sees unhappiness as fundamentally subjective, but the causes vary depending upon the theory: we suffer because of dysfunctional family systems, absent or poor parenting, early childhood trauma, environmental stressors such as a lack of safety, and so on. Yet where therapy tends to focus on solving immediate and specific individual problems (becoming complex and highly personalized), Buddhism seeks to address the nature of problems themselves, and thus its techniques serve everyone. The more we explore, understand, and even come to appreciate our own self-destructive mental attitudes, the more control we gain over our minds. As we train ourselves to look inward, we will understand how we continually thwart our own well-being by engaging the feelings and thoughts that cause us pain. And by teaching our minds how to engage and resolve destructive feelings and thoughts head-on whenever they occur, we can increasingly, and perhaps even permanently, alleviate suffering from our lives and realize our true potential.

This book is a set of ideas and tools so we can begin the *gradual process* of becoming happier by directly engaging our problems. This happiness is much different from, and independent of, the external pleasures we usually seek to make ourselves feel better, such as drugs, medications, exercise, diet, sex, relationships, career, food, travel. Each of these may make us happy for a time, but they are only temporary salves. They almost never solve our problems, and they often end up creating more. However, while there are no guarantees in life, I will make the following promise: if you read this book, contemplate its ideas, and sincerely practice the techniques it offers, even if you don't try or agree with everything, you will derive a long-term, practical benefit that will help you alleviate your own suffering and that you can rely on for the rest of your life.

A BUDDHIST PSYCHOLOGY

The ideas presented in this book are rooted in over twenty-five hundred years of experimentation, testing, application, and success. For this reason alone, they are worth paying attention to. In the premodern era, Buddhism found success in such diverse cultures as India, Sri Lanka, Afghanistan, southern Russia, Japan, Indonesia, China, Tibet, and other cultures I believe one major reason for this is because Buddhism uncovers universal truths about the nature of mind. While these truths are central to the Buddhist religion and to Buddhist spiritual practice, their application and usefulness extend to everyone. They have long been recognized as a system of psychology, and as a psychotherapist, I've used Buddhist ideas about mind with my therapy patients with great success. Interestingly, even though modern psychology is comparatively very, very new — as a field, it is still in a state of change, of finding itself — many people, particularly in North America and Europe, feel much more comfortable dealing with their emotional problems employing this new system of thought. This book, then, seeks to present the essence of Buddhist teachings about the nature of mind, or Buddhist psychology, so that anyone can use them. There is no religious dogma to follow, and no need, or desire, for the reader to become Buddhist in order to apply these ideas and achieve a highly purposeful and rich life.

When we experience emotional pain or suffering, both modern therapy and Buddhism urge us to engage our difficulties, rather than run from them, deflect them, or cover them up. Only by dealing with our problems can we solve them. Yet, modern psychology and Buddhism approach problems in subtle yet crucially different ways. Therapists tend to treat problems as obstacles to happiness; we work with therapists to get rid of our problems so we can get back to enjoying our lives. Much of Buddhist thought encourages us to embrace our problems like old friends. It even encourages us to seek out our problems as a way to train our minds and to break free from the control of our disturbing (but sometimes unseen) emotions. Great practitioners like the Dalai Lama even claim to enjoy problems because, like our best friends, problems honestly and accurately reflect ourselves back to us. There is no clearer measure of our interior health than the nature of our problems.

This shift in perspective regarding our problems is one of the keys to this book — as we develop a different relationship with our problems, we solve them in new ways, and we truly become able to heal ourselves. To clarify, being "friends" with our problems does not mean we accept them at face value or wallow in them. Rather, we use the opportunities problems offer us to think in new, more successful ways, thus becoming freer, happier, and more mentally balanced. As we become more aware and develop our understanding of the mind, we will begin to notice that we have actually already "befriended" our problems, or our negative emotions, and we have often let them become a bad influence on us. These friends control us and lead us to make the wrong choices. In our minds as in life, some friendships are destructive. For example, those "friends" who entice or cajole us into bar-hopping every night and into always drinking more than we should. As some already know, there are "friends" who willingly aid and abet our addictions and worst tendencies. These types of friends may flatter us, and promise us all sorts of fun, but they are dishonest. A true friend honors and encourages our best self, and they will work at saving us from self-destruction, even if that means being difficult. So it is with our problems. They are difficult, but they are honest like good friends should be, and they provide the exact support and help we need to liberate ourselves from the control of our negative emotions.

Another important aspect to the Buddhist approach is that all happiness and suffering is a *state of mind*. We always have the power to heal ourselves because the only way to eliminate suffering and achieve lasting happiness is by changing the way we relate to our mind. Nothing in the external world can effect this type of positive change — no career achievement, material possession, social status, or loving relationship. Make no mistake: all of the above can support a happier lifestyle. They can assist us in having a more directed and successful life. Nor do we need to renounce our creature comforts and live like a monk in order to heal our mind. However, pleasures and worldly accomplishments can easily become distractions, and we often treat them as ends in themselves. When this happens, we often find that our sense of satisfaction diminishes and our unhappiness increases.

Lasting happiness requires a long-term approach. We can't permanently prevent or alleviate the conditions that lead to depression, anxiety, addictions, or eating disorders solely by taking this pill or changing that behavior. Rather, we need to develop a deep awareness of the way our problems arise, their root causes, and then we need to train ourselves in how to cope with them every time they come up. Like physical exercise, this is something we need to do throughout our life, every day, if we want to stay in shape. There are no shortcuts. Nor is this about our religious beliefs or backgrounds. It is nothing more or less than gradually evolving an awareness of our self-destructive tendencies from the inside out.

Some readers might be thinking about now, "This sounds like a lot of work. My problems aren't actually all that bad. I'm sure if I just adopted a more positive attitude, I could solve them better." Indeed, modern therapy often encourages us to cultivate a positive, optimistic approach in order to minimize and overcome our problems, and I certainly believe we should feel self-confident that we can handle any problem life throws our way. I don't disagree with this, but I do find it incomplete and insufficient. Here's why: If we are ignorant of botany, and don't know how to distinguish plants, our happy garden will, eventually, be overcome by weeds. We will spend all our time frantically pulling up the plants we don't like, and lasting happiness will elude us; if we never figure out how to stop weeds from growing, they will always keep appearing. In other words, a plucky attitude may keep us going, but it doesn't solve the underlying issue, which Buddhism maintains is rooted in our very conception of self and mind. How we think about our mind and its functions is faulty, and so we have developed habitual mental patterns and conditioning that, if left unchanged, will always undermine and overwhelm a mere positive attitude. It also means that solving any individual problem amounts to nothing more than a quick fix, unless the root cause of our human dilemma is also tackled head-on.

And what is our human dilemma? That the *nature of life is problematic*. Problems are not an exception; they are the norm. The world offers recurring and seemingly endless conundrums for us to deal with. These dilemmas arise for each and every human being. And they arise again and again. We cannot stop problems, but we can end our suffering, and we can achieve true, lasting happiness by understanding the nature of our mind and changing the way we approach our emotional struggles.

A BUDDHIST THERAPIST

Some years after opening my private psychotherapy practice in Santa Cruz, I was driving with my primary spiritual mentor, Lama Zopa Rinpoche. Accompanying us was Choden Rinpoche, an elder lama (a title usually reserved for a Tibetan Buddhist teacher, typically a monk or nun) who is one of Lama Zopa's teachers. I was driving these two esteemed teachers to my new office in order to consecrate it. Consecrating new buildings when moving into a new location is a typical practice among many traditional Eastern cultures. As we were driving, Lama Zopa, almost out of nowhere, made a statement that would shake the foundation of my professional life. He was casually asking me about my work when, deliberately, he stated, "You know, if you're just helping people feel better, *there is no benefit.*"

At that moment, for me, the floor dropped out. I almost felt dizzy. I saw a flash before my inner eye of every client I had worked with for the past several years. I saw the numerous teenagers in crisis, parents in distress, couples in tears, and individuals in confusion and pain. And I wondered to myself, "If there is no benefit in just helping people feel better, had I been beneficial *at all, ever, in my professional work?*" I felt distraught. The more I thought about Lama Zopa's statement, the more quitting my profession seemed to be my only recourse. But what did Rinpoche really mean? Lama Zopa's statement, for me, seemed to catalyze the dialogue about the fundamental difference between modern psychology and Buddhism. While we continued with the consecration, the impact of Lama Zopa's statement resonated and percolated within my being for months to come. In fact, I continue to be both guided and troubled by it.

Immediately afterward, I thought long and hard about Lama Zopa's use of the word "benefit." I knew that Rinpoche was speaking to me personally and was not necessarily making a sweeping judgment of Western therapy or modern therapists. For a Buddhist master like Lama Zopa, the concept of "benefit" has a very particular definition. "Benefit" in the Buddhist context means *lasting, long-term, enduring* mental benefit. As a mental health professional I was, by definition, concerned with my clients' mental well-being. As a Buddhist, Rinpoche was challenging me as to whether or not I was focused upon my clients' *lasting, long-term, enduring* mental health.

I felt that Rinpoche was wondering if I was making a stand by being true to my beliefs about the true causes of happiness, learned from my years of study in Buddhist thought. In other words, was I being courageous and authentic to my values and philosophy of happiness? Sadly, at that time, the answer was less than a resounding "yes."

Since then, I have steadily recalibrated my therapeutic approach as a way of "getting to yes." I first began studying Buddhism when I was twenty-one and attended an intensive, one-month meditation and teaching retreat at Kopan Monastery in Nepal. That was in 1975, and I continued studying and retreating until I left Nepal in 1988, some fourteen years later. Upon settling back in the United States, I have until this day — despite raising three children and pursuing a career in psychology — continued to study with Tibetan Buddhist masters and to engage in Buddhist practice. I have also studied and practiced psychotherapy since the 1990s, graduating from university in 1992 and opening my private practice in 1994. It's safe to say that merging these two psychological practices or systems in order to bring *lasting, long-term, enduring* mental health benefits to others has been my life's work and mission, and it is the purpose of this book.

MIND TRAINING
AND THOUGHT TRANSFORMATION

In this very moment we have the potential power within our own mind to transform our ordinary, mundane, problem-riddled life into a life of ease and contentment. We can transform the nature of our problems, and thus get rid of our problems. But for this method to be effective it needs to be based in an accurate understanding of how problems arise, their causes, and their makeup. We must strive to understand our mind and how problems arise so that we can then develop the skill to transform these endless problems into happiness.

How do we develop this skill? Through practice and training.

Understanding is not enough. The idea of training the mind may sound a bit foreign or new. Remember Jack LaLanne? He changed the world of fitness when he began hosting his television show in 1951. Prior to that, the idea of toning and training the body was reserved for a few "muscle men," athletes, and soldiers. LaLanne promoted the idea that anyone could get extraordinary results from training their bodies, and since then it's become common practice. For example, in 1951, how many ordinary people were running twenty-six-mile marathons? Today, tens of thousands of people train regularly to develop their bodies and accomplish athletic feats that were pretty much unheard of fifty or sixty years ago. Like the body, the mind too can be trained. In fact, I believe the body has limitations on what it can achieve no matter how much we train, but the mind's potential is unlimited.

In contrast with the West, mind training has a rich history in the Buddhist tradition. It reaches back all the way to the Buddha, who created these principles and techniques, which have been preserved through an unbroken lineage of practitioners to the present day. Buddhists train the mind to increase its discipline, strength, and discernment. An untrained mind is like a young puppy, running wild through the house, soiling the furniture, and, despite its playfulness, upsetting everyone and ruling the roost. Training the mind is also how you acquire the skillful discernment to understand the nature of your problems and solve them effectively. As this occurs, you get mentally stronger, literally more fit and capable. There is a Tibetan proverb that says, "Don't put the load of a dzo on a cow." A "dzo" is a female yak, and yaks can carry a lot more than cows. In other words, you can't expect an untrained mind to handle life's biggest problems. But like the proverbial ninety-eight-pound weakling from the 1950s, you can train yourself by using small problems as dumbbells to build your mental muscles until there's nothing in the world that can bully you.

As such, this book is organized and focused on getting you training right away. The first chapter discusses the nature of problems, and chapter 2 describes the essential techniques that you will use to train your mind. These techniques are used throughout and can be applied to any situation. At first, though, honestly and appropriately assess your own capabilities, and focus initially on those easier problems you feel ready to handle. You'll soon see results and find you can tackle "weightier" issues each time.

The next five chapters (chapters 3 through 7) look in more depth at the central Buddhist concepts that inform this approach. These chapters present our faulty thoughts and how they are transformed so that we can achieve lasting happiness. We will examine the nature of mind, our disturbing emotions, how we create our own (self-defeating) stories, the lessons of impermanence, and the true nature of self. In each of these chapters, I provide more exercises that you can use to expand and improve your training.

Chapter 8 looks at the various distractions and ways that we often undermine our own efforts at self-improvement, and chapter 9 ends with the most important practice of all, compassion and goodheartedness. When we understand the real culprit that prevents us from being fulfilled — the "not-knowing" of how the mind functions — we cultivate a transformative compassion for ourselves and others. Through these investigations, we learn that the mind is lucid and pure. We learn that the myriad disturbing emotions — like fear, self-loathing, obsessive thinking, agitation, anxiety, depression, and so on — are like clouds that move across the sky of the mind. And we learn that, through training, we can cultivate a point of view that is less "sticky" to our emotions, and thus continually develop a more refined state of happiness.

The concept of using problems to get rid of problems may sound new. It is interesting to note, however, that if we honestly assess our own good qualities, those we have developed over our lifetime, we might be surprised to see that they have invariably arisen through meeting hardship, pain, and struggle. Our problems and struggles are, in fact, our own best guide when we apply the right perspective. It is our perspective that is the problem, not the external events and interactions that come our way.

We are a society of quick fixes, but when it comes to happiness, easy answers don't suffice; they only address our problems at a symptomatic level. We must have the courage and patience not only to become familiar with our underlying neuroses but to engage, enjoy, celebrate, and appreciate them. Then our problems change shape, or to use an analogy expressed by some ancient Buddhist masters, "They become ornaments we can wear." We need to slow down and take an honest look at our unhelpful thoughts and emotions. The results will surprise us. No matter how serious and intransigent your problems seem, *The Misleading Mind* will prove transformational — the first step on a long but fulfilling journey to your own best self.

CHAPTER ONE

So, What's the Problem?

When I was nineteen years old, I once worked for my brother-in-law, Scott, when he was the manager of the installation department at a vertical blind company. A hard-working Midwesterner, Scott had big goals; he wanted to be successful and move up the corporate ladder. As for myself and my best friend and co-worker, Dave, we were in it for the short-term gain: some extra cash to pay for weekends spent partying and surfing. Dave had long, stringy blonde surfer hair. I had an afro. Together we wore the uniform of the sixties counterculture: baggy blue jeans, blue surf shoes, and a solid-color pocket T-shirt. Dave always looked like he had just climbed out of bed, having slept the night in his clothes.

One morning when we were receiving our daily orders from Scott, he asked us to mind the office for a few minutes while he ran out to do an errand. Every now and then, the phone rang with customers calling with questions or complaints. Then I went to gather the supplies we needed to fill the day's orders, leaving Dave to answer the telephone. Of course, asking Dave to man the phone was a bit like asking Lindsay Lohan to watch your kids. You can't expect things to go smoothly.

As Scott and I both returned to the office simultaneously from separate entrances, we saw Dave clasping the phone to his ear, one hand at his hip. He was shouting at the top of his lungs: "Lady! *Lady!* You think *you've* got problems? Lady, *EVERYBODY'S GOT PROBLEMS!*" Dave then slammed the phone down, looked at Scott, whose face was ashen, and said, "Can you believe these people!?"

Dave had just delivered one of my first and most profound lessons in life, and it was the same lesson the Buddha taught in his first sermon twenty-five hundred years ago, after he'd spent years in meditation and asceticism: the nature of life is suffering. Everybody's got problems.

The real question is: What do we do with them?

THE FOUR NOBLE TRUTHS

When the Buddha first experienced enlightenment, he was initially reluctant to share his experience. This was not because he was selfish, wanting to keep his profound insights to himself. No, he was reluctant to speak because what he had experienced was beyond the convention of words. He knew that even if he could explain it, no one could truly understand his message if they did not also experience it themselves.

However, many people were struck by his depth of serenity, control, and warmth. Finally, the Buddha decided that sharing his experience and wisdom was the right thing to do, but even then, he believed there was only a small chance that he could have a positive impact on a few people. Thus he gave his first teaching, typically referred to as the "Four Noble Truths." These are, slightly rephrased:

1. Life means suffering. Life is in the nature of suffering.
2. Suffering arises from clinging or attachment that comes about through wrong perception. Suffering is not random; it has a cause.
3. Suffering can be overcome. There is a blissful state of being that is free from suffering.
4. There is a way out, a path, and here it is.

The first truth he spoke about was the "Truth of Suffering." This states that every being experiences physical and emotional pain. At any moment, things can shift, and we have no real control to prevent pain and problems from arising. Nothing lasts, including our joys and pleasures, our friends and loved ones, our attainments and achievements, and so we are "set up" for disappointment. Everything is impermanent.

When I first heard the teachings on the Four Noble Truths, it concerned me that the Buddha called suffering a *truth.* He didn't say it was a concept, or a principle, or even a theory. Like the truths of America's Declaration of Independence, suffering was "self-evident." It disturbed me because, if it was a "truth," I couldn't simply reject it if I didn't like the idea. Humans don't float or fly in the air by "rejecting" the truth of gravity. We aren't free to accept gravity if we like it or ignore it if we don't. If suffering was a *truth,* then like my dealings with gravity, I was accountable for understanding it and obliged to contend with it.

The Second Noble Truth explains the main cause of suffering: our desires, or more specifically, our attachment to what we desire and our misunderstanding of how things really exist. Buddha noticed that people usually treat problems like random occurrences, and they typically misunderstand the nature or cause of the problems they experience. By understanding that all difficulties have a cause and assigning them the correct cause, we can begin to permanently become free of the suffering that results. In essence, we cause our own problems by seeking, desiring, or relying on transient, external things to make us happy. This extends not just to stuff — like cars, jobs, romantic relationships, family, income, and so on — but to our concepts. We become attached to our own sense of self, and to seeing the world in a certain way, and this leads to suffering.

The Third Noble Truth says that, once we subdue and uproot the causes of our problems, there is a state of being that is eternally peaceful, joyful, and free of struggle. The very absence of the causes and effects of suffering leaves us with a positive state of well-being. Then, in the Fourth Noble Truth, the Buddha outlines the way to achieve this. Just wanting to be happy is not the path to happiness. All living creatures wish to be happy, and all living creatures spend every moment of their lives seeking happiness. And yet, the achievement of a lasting state of well-being continues to elude all of us. Why? Because we do not actually understand the way out. But there are correct theories and methods that work. Permanently.

CRUISING ALONG

We could rephrase the first two noble truths, in part, as: nothing lasts, and pursuing pleasures does not stop the pain of this. Nothing illustrates this better than life aboard a cruise ship.

My mother is in her late eighties and has been on her own since my dad died several years ago. My father worked hard as a small businessman, and he made enough money so that when he retired my mother and he could indulge in the activity they loved most — travel. As they aged and became weary of airplanes and packing and unpacking, they spent more and more of their leisure time on cruise ships. Eventually, they spent almost five months a year cruising the seven seas.

After my father died it seemed therapeutic for my mom to continue cruising. My mother stayed in the best cabin — in a penthouse about the size of four normal cabins. It came with a butler, a large balcony, floor-to-ceiling windows, and an unending array of canapés and snacks like caviar, lobster, crab, pâté, collector's wines, and $300 bottles of champagne — whatever one wanted. Her itinerary included five months of cruising to captivating ports around the world, and my mom was riding in the very peak of worldly delight. If this didn't help her ease her pain, what could?

And yet, my mother was fairly miserable. She was frequently distressed because she was desperately trying to keep her life together: looking good to the other passengers, making sure she was sitting at the proper table in the dining room, and moving about the ship despite her poor health. She no longer got off the ship at the various ports because, she said, "I've been here before." She could not play bridge because her memory was so bad. But most of all, she missed my dad. Nothing on the cruise ship could stop that; in fact, I suspect the cruise ship only served as a constant reminder. She barely touched all the great food that was available to her. Instead, she snacked on cookies and had no appetite for dinner.

Perhaps this isn't surprising. Dealing with death is one of the biggest problems we'll ever face, and yet my mother was far from the only unhappy person on the cruise ship. My wife and I accompanied my mom for a portion of her cruise, to help care for her, and it seemed that no one we met was free of complaints. All one had to do was sit down and chat with someone for a few minutes, and inevitably the grumbling would start: about a particular waiter's ineptitude; the lack of lathering quality of the new bathing soap; the weather being too hot, too cold, or too cloudy; or the ports on this segment being too boring. It went on and on and on.

Of course, people's degree of complaints varied, and perhaps many were carrying sorrows and problems equal to my mother's.

Yet very soon, my wife and I felt the same way: we couldn't wait to get off the ship and back home. But why? If a cruise ship doesn't define easy, problem-free living, what does? The reason I was anxious to get off that ship, and the reason everyone on it was wrestling with some level of dissatisfaction, was because we were faced with an uneasy truth: no amount of pleasure and ease could help us escape the problems that inherently exist within our own minds. Contentment and satisfaction can only come from inside: my mother and father were happy to cruise together because they were happy before they got on the ship. They didn't need the cruise to make them happy. After that experience accompanying my mother, I understood the expression "too much of a good thing." After a certain level of saturation, pleasures just begin to create a sense of greater longing and discontent. Being on the ship for over a month was like eating an entire cheesecake instead of a proper dinner — I felt bloated.

The Buddha understood the human impulse to avoid suffering by denying one's pain and distracting oneself with what feels good. But he also observed the truth that such efforts will never achieve lasting satisfaction and happiness. The typical way humans pursue contentment is flawed. We cannot, it seems, avoid our problems, even when we live in the lap of luxury, because our external circumstances do not truly affect the nature of our problems. That's because, according to the Buddha, our problems are caused by our misperception of the nature of reality and the nature of our mind.

THE INADEQUACY OF THINGS

I like to think of the Buddha's First Noble Truth as the Truth of Problems, or what we could call Dave's First Noble Truth. Life means dealing with problems; some are bigger and some are smaller, but you can't escape them. Look around and you can see that everything humans have ever manufactured was made either to avoid a potential problem or to take care of a problem we already have. Examine your living room or office. Every object can be seen as an ally against problems. We have things to avoid physical aches: a phone headset to wear on your ear, a foot rest to avoid leg cramps while sitting, an adjustable keyboard tray for typing at the correct height. Our computers solve a whole host of problems: with email, we no longer have to mail letters; spellcheck has replaced the need for a dictionary; I can write and edit and communicate faster. Lamps solve the problem of the dark. Pants protect my legs from cold and weather and the embarrassment of showing my legs in public.

But you know the freaky thing? Every one of these problem-solving aids will become its own problem. Why? Everything changes. Nothing lasts or stays the same. When the weather turns warm, my pants can be too hot, and then they get dirty and I have to wash them, and then they wear out and I have to replace them. My computer software must be continually updated; if my power cord short-circuits, all my work could be lost. Indeed, I could shock myself from handling the plug incorrectly. How many of us can't stand to be without our cell phones, but then curse when the phone rings at dinnertime, or when we're about to go to asleep and people just *won't leave us alone?*

If you watch TV, you know that every single commercial advertises a product that either helps avoid a problem or alleviates one that exists. Advertisers are smart. They understand the pervasiveness of problems. Lama Yeshe often used to say that "advertisers are the real social psychologists, since they really understand how consumers' minds work."

Yet not only don't external comforts provide lasting relief to our emotional pains, they don't even provide lasting relief for our everyday practical and physical problems.

THE THREE CONDITIONS

Problems themselves can be grouped into three categories. Buddhism typically calls them the Three Sufferings, but I prefer the Three Conditions:

1. We are continually experiencing physical discomfort or pain.
2. Life is always changing and unpredictable.
3. We are ignorant of the true nature of reality.

We will look at all three of these situations throughout the book, for in training our mind, we are seeking to solve each of them. Note that these Three Conditions are, slightly recast, the same as the Three Destructive Emotions discussed in chapter 4.

Physical Pain

It's easy enough to see that we experience physical pain or discomfort throughout the day, whether it is hunger pangs, thirst, stubbing a toe, tightness in the back while sitting, colds and hay fever, dust in our eyes, smog in our throats, burning our tongue on our soup, or having a hang nail. In fact, our body is constantly in need of adjustment. If we stay in any one position too long, we have to shift because we start to cramp up and ache. We may think that there is no way to avoid this type of pain, but we will see that, for true masters, even physical pain can be controlled in the mind. The first condition is something that comes about, we could say, just by virtue of the fact that we have a body. In traditional Buddhist descriptions the body is referred to as a bundle of pain. Indeed, our body is a "bundle of nerves" that when barely touched can bring excruciating pain. Step on a tack, eat the wrong food, get a bug in your eye, sit on a hard floor — all result in pain.

Everything Changes

We live as if everything were static, but life is fluid and unpredictable. (This concept will be explored more thoroughly in chapters 5 and 6.) There are many ramifications of this idea, but the main one is that because change is constant, we are never secure. We are always vulnerable. Nothing stays the same, and at any moment, really, anything can happen. Every day we are older, and at any moment death could come. We really have no control over what will happen to us in the next hour, minute, or second. When we hear of sudden tragedies, we are always thankful it wasn't us, until the day it is us. Our health can change in a split second.

Further, as I've said above, our external world is always throwing us curveballs and new problems to solve, and our moods and emotions are always shifting and outside our control. We may wish to control them, and we often spend a lot of effort trying to, but our success rate is extremely low. Thus, to solve this problem, we eventually have to accept the unfixed nature of the world and ourselves.

Ignorance

The third condition is, simply put, that *we are ignorant of the nature of reality*. This condition is pervasive. In essence, our biggest problem is that we don't understand the true nature of our problem. This can be one of the hardest Buddhist teachings to understand, and I will look at it more closely in chapters 3 and 7, where we look at the nature of mind and the nature of self. But in everyday terms, it's fairly easy to see. When we are suffering terrible emotional pain and seek to feel better by indulging in pleasures, we aren't solving the nature of our problem. When we try to control our fate, our circumstances in life, or even our mood, this displays our ignorance over the impermanent nature of life. We might recognize that we can't control the world, but if we really take a deep look into our inner workings, we'll see that we can't control our own happiness either. Despite our desires, we cannot just "turn on a switch" within ourselves and make that happen.

As much or more than anything else, the mind-training techniques in this book are meant to address this ignorance. With a deep, lived understanding of the true nature of our problems, all problems can be solved, for it is out of ignorance that all problems arise. It should also be said that this "ignorance" is not about intelligence. It's not about how smart one is, nor is it about willfully "not knowing" a painful truth. It is ignorance of the nature of existence. Unless we understand this, we cannot understand how to exercise free choice, we cannot transform our minds to their full potential, and we cannot truly help others or ourselves.

CASE EXAMPLE: HIGH-ANXIETY CARL

Carl was a self-admitted "control freak with a Type-A personality." A good day for Carl — which is not his real name, as I have used pseudonyms for all client stories — was a day when Trisha, his wife, kept the house in order, he got all the green lights in his drive to work, and his clinic ran without interruptions to his schedule. Carl was not untypical. He had a lot of anxiety, and his happiness always depended on how well he managed his anxiety. And so long as people did things his way, he felt he could do a good job keeping his anxiety under control.

Carl is a great example of how suffering is always caused internally and of how lasting happiness depends on changing how we think, not managing the world or others. Like most "control freaks," Carl was actually the one being manipulated — by his own anxiety. Carl was one of those guys who tried to control every potential difficulty before it arose. He expected problems everywhere, and so, of course, his life was full of them. He was a guy who mistakenly believed that "if he covered the world with leather, he would be free of the pain of the world's thorns," as the Buddhist saying goes.

When Carl and Trisha first came to me, Carl was looking for support to help his wife become more efficient, less messy, and better organized. But this didn't fool me. Carl's "problem" wasn't with Trisha, it was with himself, and my job would be to convince Carl that the answer to the hazards of the world's thorns wasn't to cover the world with leather, but to cover your feet with leather sandals.

Carl and Trisha argued a lot. They had marital problems. The more Carl dictated how their home and lives should be run, the more Trisha resisted. From Carl's point of view, Trisha's "spaciness" was the problem. From Trisha's point of view, Carl's obsessive organizing was the problem. They both saw the problem "out there," located in the other person, rather than rooted in their own anxieties. From a Buddhist psychological perspective this incorrect view of the outer world as being controllable and predictable is a source of a great many psychological disorders.

We investigated what Carl was looking for when he compulsively attempted to control his environment, and he would say, "When everything is in order, then I can relax." Yet Carl had not really thought about the possibility, or the dilemma, of what happens if everything cannot be in order. I asked him how frequently he was at ease, not struggling for order. He admitted that it was only a few hours a week. So I asked him: "For the most part, then, who is in control: Carl or anxiety?" He had to admit that anxiety was ruling him most of the time.

Trisha was also at the mercy of anxiety, which was running her life. In fact, it was her anxiety about Carl's anxiety that made her "spacey," or unable to focus, because she was distracted by her worry about upsetting Carl. Eventually, both Carl and Trisha agreed to join forces in fighting anxiety rather than fighting each other, which is what they had been doing. By fighting anxiety, they were each agreeing to take personal responsibility for their own reactions or negative emotions, rather than blaming the other for creating them. More importantly, they were working to eliminate the root cause of anxiety itself. They came to realize that fighting and resolving particular conflicts — that a carton of milk was left out on the counter, the toothpaste cap was left off the toothpaste tube, there was dust on the windowsill — would be endless. These incidents were only symptoms or conditions. The only enduring solution was to confront their agitated mindset.

At this point, I want to caution that the modern psychological and Buddhist perspectives have fundamental differences around the idea of internal accountability. While this is easily and commonly understood as "personal responsibility," this isn't a matter of replacing "other-blaming" with "self-blaming." We will look more closely at this below and in later chapters, but in essence, in the Buddhist perspective, one stops *all* misplaced or ignorant blame and learns to put the blame where it belongs: on our misperception of things and of our self and on the habitual, compulsive reactions those misperceptions lead us to take. Simply apply a wise, observing perspective to the workings of one's own mind and emotions, clearly and honestly, without prejudice or old assumptions.

In Carl and Trisha's case, this "wise philosophy" began at the basic level of being mindful whenever they were being "tricked" into blaming their partner for their unhappiness. If Trisha left the milk carton out, so that Carl had warm milk when he ate his morning cereal, Carl was faced with a choice: he could respond in his old habitual, agitated manner or in a new, mindful manner. Warm milk was not the problem, or the real culprit causing agitation. The warm milk was merely an outer condition. If he needed cold milk to be happy, then his environment was controlling him. Could he deal with warm milk, or any unexpected event, and cope without agitation? If warm milk with his cereal was not a threat to his emotional well-being, then where was the problem? Without agitation, there is no enemy. And thus, without agitation there was no conflict with Trisha.

SEEING THE BIG PICTURE

Sometimes people tell me that when they begin to open themselves up to problems, they become not just somewhat problem-oriented but problem-saturated. As they begin to address the source of problems in their own mind, and to see the world differently, their impression is that things actually become worse. This sense of things getting worse is not so much *the result* of looking at problems but *the manner in which* we look at problems. Sometimes, people will interpret the message as "Everything exists inside of me. Therefore, it is all my fault." Well, in the long run, our pain and happiness are in our own hands; I do not believe there is a god, savior, knight in shining armor, or angel of love that is going to bestow eternal happiness upon us. However, by recognizing that "problems" arise within us, that doesn't mean we are somehow wrong or deficient, or that we should identify with our problems as being who we are. We do have problems, but this does not mean we *are* problems. We believe our problem and our self are the same. This is looking at problems in the wrong way, in a damaging way. Remember, according to Buddhism, *everyone* has problems, and everyone has the *same* problem: the suffering of attachment based on our ignorance of the true nature of mind.

In order to solve this universal, existential "problem," we must open ourselves to our entire inner experience. We do so not with fear or intimidation but with curiosity and openness — with the eager, objective, nonjudgmental curiosity of an archaeologist or an astronomer exploring the boundaries of space and the nature of life. We must look at all aspects of ourself, without worrying if they are "good" or "bad." If we only focus on what we like or don't like — choosing to only recognize our good traits or to always blame ourselves for every wrong — then we are equally blind, and we close the door on discovering our utterly remarkable, astonishing, and undiscovered strengths. The fact is, we often avoid seeing or admitting our less savory qualities, and we can find it very difficult to accept that the source of our anger and unhappiness is always within. If someone is rude to us, even abusive, isn't our reaction *their* fault? No. Like the milk in Carl's story, they are the condition, but not the cause. However, the further truth is that we also need to evaluate our own capacities and strengths. Problems come in all shapes and sizes, and very few of us can handle each equally well. What we can handle depends upon our capacity. We can increase our capacity through training.

Further, while this book focuses on the practical application of these ideas in everyday life, this is a true "spiritual" practice that is intended to create a life that is meaningful, rich, and extraordinary. Investigating the nature of our minds is about uncovering and developing the unlimited potential of our minds. As I mentioned earlier, this state of mind is so remarkable that anything compared to it is unfulfilling. Just because we are not fully living in that state of mind does not mean it does not exist nor that we cannot live there every moment of our lives. In fact, that wonderful state is our birthright, and we should claim it. Not doing so is like being a scuba diver and only snorkeling in an inflatable swimming pool.

The Tibetan word *nang-pa* means "Buddhist," and it has an interesting etymology. *Nang* means inside, in, or inner. *Pa* is an identifier meaning "person" or "living being." So, in Tibetan, "Buddhist" means an Inner Being. Being an Inner Being indicates our point of focus. An insider understands that all of one's myriad, seemingly endless problems and conflicts arise from inside, and that all of one's happiness, contentment, and success arise from inside. Being an insider is a point of view and a strategy for living. It is an expression of faith in the unlimited potential of humanity's internal makeup.

To be a spiritual person in this way has nothing to do with one's religion. Insiders can be Jewish, Christian, Buddhist, Hindu, Muslim, or agnostic. Inner beings exist everywhere, among every walk of life: washing your car, serving your food, delivering your new couch, selling your house, protecting your street, designing the next microchip or vaccine, waiting for a handout at the stoplight, sitting in a hermitage, or sitting on Wall Street. You, too, are an "inner being" when you seek emotional balance through inner health.

"PEOPLE ARE AT DIFFERENT LEVELS"

In the 1970s and early 1980s, Lama Yeshe was the head abbot of the Kopan Monastery in Nepal and the inspiration behind the powerful one-month meditation course held every winter on the monastery grounds. Sometimes we would have over two hundred foreign visitors attending the course: hippies, scholars, dharma bums, seekers, and the curious. For a number of years, my wife and I had pivotal roles managing the courses, since we were two of just a few resident Westerners living at the monastery.

One day I was fed up with the behavior of many of the participants, who were violating the strict rules of the course. We were hearing of people leaving the "hill" and going to town to get a good meal and a shower, smoke some hashish, and then slip back into the monastery. I was complaining to Lama Yeshe about the people who were sneaking out, and he listened patiently to my "holier than thou" whining. When I finished with my rant, he calmly looked up at me from his seat in his living quarters and softly said, both as a statement of empathy and a command to me, "People are at different levels, dear."

What he said was so simple but revealed so much. Lama Yeshe, like most Buddhist teachers, can hold in one hand our great potential while in the other maintaining a realistic view of our current capabilities. It is a unique perspective that is both empathetic and hopeful. Lama's declaration became, for me, another priceless statement that still rings in my ears and my spirit and has guided me in much of my counseling and consulting work.

In other words, we need to begin with a realistic view of our situation in life. It takes courage to open ourselves up to all of our qualities, both difficult and inspiring, that dwell within our being. If at any point you find you've left the "hill" for a good meal and a shower, don't beat yourself up. Don't compare yourself to others. Just recognize what's happened and keep trying. Having limits and blind spots is part of being human; acknowledge any blindness and attempt to keep your eyes open next time. We need to take the "middle way." We can take holidays in order to refresh ourselves to return to work. It is not through ignorance that we become stronger and liberated — it is through wisdom, knowledge, and openness.

MEDITATION EXERCISE: YOU CAN COUNT ON IT

This is a foundation exercise that I recommend you use before all the other exercises in the book. Each morning, before the day gets into full gear, sit in a quiet spot. You can sit cross-legged or in a comfortable chair; what's important is that your spine is straight. A straight spine allows the breath to move freely and naturally and also facilitates the mind's staying clear and focused.

Gently close your eyes and tilt your head downward very, very slightly. Allow the breathing to happen naturally, without force or control. After getting settled, bring the focus of your mind upon the breath going in and out of your nostrils. As the breath is exhaled and then inhaled, repeat to yourself "one." With the next exhalation and inhalation, "two." There is no other focus than the breath and the recitation of the number quietly in the background of your mind as you inhale. The aim is to remain focused upon the breath until you get to the number ten. At that point, count backward to one. Start over. Do three sets of ten.

If you find that your mind wanders — and it will do that a lot, particularly when you first engage in this practice — you must start over from one. You might find that you can only get to five or six before you find yourself thinking about breakfast, phone calls you've got to make, or last night's TV shows. That's okay. It will happen, and when it does, start over. At first it may take many minutes, or several sessions, to count to ten and back three times without losing focus, but eventually this will get easier and easier, and the benefits will become more apparent.

CHAPTER TWO

Training the Untrained Mind

Mind training is essential to Buddhism. In essence, it is the path the Buddha advocated in his Fourth Noble Truth. And yet, as I've said, mind training is not necessarily a religious or spiritual practice. It does not rest on accepting certain religious beliefs or adopting particular terminology. It can be used successfully as an entirely secular practice, or it can be incorporated as a deliberate spiritual practice within any religion, whether you are Christian, Muslim, Hindu, Jewish, or something else. You can be a business-person, schoolteacher, or a stay-at-home mom or dad and still prac-tice mind training. Naturally, the ideas behind mind training, or the explanations of mind the Buddha presented in his first three Noble Truths, are equally essential no matter our place in life. Training and theory go hand in hand. So, as you read the rest of the book, keep practicing the mind training methods this chapter describes, and as you practice, keep reading to steadily improve your under-standing and success.

As we begin, I want to share a wonderful and amusing histor-ical anecdote that captures what the practice is all about and how transformative it can be. From the seventh century, Buddhism flourished in Tibet, but in the ninth century, it declined as a result of a ruthless Tibetan king who aimed to destroy Buddhism in his country. Then, in the early eleventh century, Tibetan Buddhism began a regeneration. This was marked by increased travel between Tibet and India, as key Tibetans traveled to India for instruction, and many Indian masters were invited to Tibet. Foremost of these Indian masters was Lama Atisha, a well-known scholar and practitioner who was one of India's principal teachers of mind training. Lama Atisha was invited personally by the current king to spearhead the reestablishing of Tibet's rich Buddhist cultural and religious tradition. Initially, Atisha committed to staying in Tibet for three years, but he was so well-loved by Tibetans that he remained for a total of twelve years, finally passing away in Tibet.

One reason for Atisha's long initial commitment was because travel from India to Tibet was not easy. You had to negotiate hot, disease-infested jungles, eighteen-thousand-foot Himalayan passes, and inhospitable tribes and bandits. The trip took months to prepare and months to complete, involving dangers and hardships we can barely imagine today. Among the party traveling to Tibet was Atisha's personal cook, who was known as a very difficult person to get along with. And indeed, the Tibetans found him rude, crass, and unfriendly. But even worse, the cook's terrible behavior did not merely extend to the Tibetans but even to Atisha himself. The Tibetans just could not understand why Lama Atisha would keep such an unsavory person as his cook. Wasn't travel hard enough?

However, Atisha never showed any sense of intolerance, anger, or embarrassment over his cook's behavior. Then as now, traveling can sometimes bring out the worst in people, and the Tibetans were impressed that Atisha showed only affection for the cook. Finally, though, they couldn't stand it, and they asked Atisha why he did not fire the man and send him back to India. Lama Atisha replied, "He is not just my cook; he is my teacher of patience."

With that one simple statement, Lama Atisha demonstrated to the Tibetans and to us the entire concept of transforming one's inner experience through mind training.

EMBRACING OUR PROBLEMS

It would be a mistake to interpret Lama Atisha's remark as a glib attempt at humor. He was not making the best of a bad situation. Atisha was speaking the truth: he regarded the cook as his teacher, and he deliberately chose to keep this difficult man close to him. Amazingly, Lama Atisha chose to make his life harder than it needed to be.

This exemplifies the first aspect of mind training. Rather than being another way to avoid or escape problems, mind training freely embraces problems. Not only that, as Lama Atisha indicated, we must actively seek and engage our problems, rather than wait for them. Only in this way can we learn how to avoid suffering. In his case, Lama Atisha's "problem" wasn't the cook; it was his own feelings of anger or frustration stimulated by the cook's behavior. In his response to his Tibetan traveling companions, Atisha did not deny that the cook was insufferable. Instead, he was indicating the primary thrust of mind training: it is a method of handling any emotion that disturbs us so that we retain our balance and sense of inner peace.

There are numerous techniques to help us do this, but they revolve around a few basic principles: training our mind not to be "attached to" or "influenced by" our emotions, desires, or perceptions, and learning to transform negative emotions into their positive counterparts. In Lama Atisha's case, through his cook, he was practicing replacing anger with patience.

An important distinction with mind training is that it is not "reframing" or just a faith-based feel-good trick. Therapists, for example, use reframing as a common technique in therapeutic practice, and sometimes it can be quite helpful for the client. Looking on the bright side, seeing the glass as half full, identifying the beneficial lessons in an otherwise hurtful relationship: This can be a good, positive approach. But this is not mind training, and "reframing" has limited long-term usefulness. Oftentimes, reframing can feel contrived. Someone, some other, higher authority or code of belief, tells us how to feel, and so we try, even if we lack real conviction. Reframing can sometimes be illogical; it denies the truth of one's experience. We may be asked to imagine that a person who deliberately hurt us didn't really mean to hurt us. In mind training, the intentions and motivations of others, although relevant, are not the primary focus. We are concerned with our point of view and its accompanying response.

Similarly, when a terrible accident occurs, we are sometimes asked to see it as "God's will" or "punishment for our sins" or the workings of "karma." Not only does this fail to explain events, but it overlooks the real problem: how we should deal with our feelings of grief, rage, and disbelief. I consider it "reframing" when we are asked to take the goodness of the universe on faith. Don't get me wrong: faith is important. Indeed, the reasons for events often escape human understanding, and the world is unpredictable. Ultimately, these difficult, existential truths are what mind training helps us to cope with. Ultimately, in Buddhism, mind training is a spiritual practice in the sense that its goal is to awaken our inner potential.

However, that is not where the beginner starts. Instead, we start by accepting the counterintuitive notion that we must use our problems to solve our problems. Problems provide the resistance that helps us exercise our minds. When problems appear, instead of avoiding them, we confront, understand, and eliminate all of those unhelpful emotions and thoughts that arise because of them and that have run our life since the day we were born. In truth, we are merely "retraining" the mind. Just the idea that we can change and transform our everyday existence is quite encouraging by itself. It is in this way that, in training our mind, we become our own therapist and are, by my definition, spiritual practitioners. When we work with transforming our mind at more advanced levels, we actually look forward to confronting our problems, just like Lama Atisha. Why? Because we understand that the problematic conditions of the world will never go away. It is simply the nature of life. All we can do is get better at handling them. We understand that even if we are calm and happy today, something will happen tomorrow to challenge us and throw us off. Perhaps it will be an unexpected bill, or a medical problem, or a painful buried memory lying under the surface of our conscious mind that arises at the drop of a hat...like a rear-end collision that comes out of nowhere while we sit at a red light. The rather unconventional, "in your face" Buddhist approach of mind training is to courageously confront all of our dirty little secrets and difficult emotions whenever they come up until we've changed the nature of our relationship with them. Then, instead of being bossed around by our worst tendencies and disturbed emotions, we become the boss of our own mind.

THE THREE TYPES OF INTERVENTIONS

Just as there are numerous troubles and afflictions leading to all kinds of problems, we can also say there are numerous solutions equal to these problems! Buddhist psychology offers a solution to every psychological problem, but if the particulars vary, the essence of the basic approaches remains the same. There are three general categories of interventions that deal with the upsetting emotions: blocking negative impulses, observing and releasing the emotions, and transforming negative thoughts into their positive opposites.

- While it could be said that it's impossible not to feel something, we can keep ourselves from acting on or indulging our feelings. We may be able to "block" afflictions from arising, but, once they have arisen, we seek to avoid engaging in the disturbing emotion. For example, if we have a craving for chocolate, we might lock any chocolate in a kitchen cupboard and hide the keys to the car so we cannot drive to the store. If we habitually block the fulfillment of the craving, eventually the craving will subside.

- Another general category of mind training is to face emotions directly but not identify with them. When we feel disturbed, we seek to examine the experience objectively, perceive it fully, observe it, and finally allow it to dissolve. For instance, say we are irritated with our neighbor because he has allowed his trees to grow so high they block our view. Immediately, we recognize the source of our irritation as inside ourselves, not with the neighbor or his trees. We look at the irritation directly, recognize how it arises, understand that we undermine our own happiness by engaging with the emotion, and through the power of our understanding, let the irritation go until it loses all strength over us. Then, if we still want to talk to our neighbor about trimming his trees, we can, but we will have already solved the most important problem, our irritation.

- The third broad category of mind training is an extension of the second. Instead of only watching the emotion and dissolving it, we take the further step of actually analyzing it, investigating it, and transforming the emotion by offering a positive emotion to take its place. This mind-training practice is referred to as *thought transformation*. It is, essentially, using the energy of the mind and the emotions to manifest our highest, positive qualities. Lama Atisha was famous in particular for practicing thought transformation. This practice is described in more detail below and throughout.

As I say, within these broad categories are a host of specific practices, a number of which are offered in this book. Also, to varying degrees, all mind-training techniques are interrelated. Part of becoming skillful is learning when and where to apply any particular technique, but they are all mind training.

THE POWER OF THOUGHT TRANSFORMATION

The essence of thought transformation is that problems are actually helpful to us. They are what allow us to awake to our inner potential and become mentally fit. The first two basic categories of mind-training techniques help keep our unhelpful emotions at bay, so they no longer run our life. Thought training uses our fertile emotional "manure" to actively cultivate and grow our better self. We become true gardeners, removing weeds and planting flowers. But to do this, we need courage like the samurai warrior of Japanese lore. We need to be martial artists with respect to our mental world. As His Holiness the Dalai Lama says:

> With Thought Transformation we are not developing an attitude of masochism. We are not seeking to make things more difficult for ourselves through self-flagellation or wearing a hair coat. That kind of self-hurt is self-destructive. What we are doing is cultivating an attitude where problems show up and rather than run or shun them we think, "Ah, here is another area where I am under the control of my harmful emotions. Instead of running, I'm going to open my door to my enemy and see what he has to teach me. By knowing my enemy, I can defeat him. By being interested in my enemy, I disarm him. He gets his power from my habitual, unconscious reaction to him. Now, I'm going to develop a different relationship with my enemy. When I

do not hate my enemy, there is no longer an 'enemy,' only information remains."

This is how problems help! We create a different kind of relationship with our problems, and so a whole new universe opens for us. When we are anxious, irritated, covetous, or bewildered, our disturbing emotions are obscuring the true nature of reality. Once we see the true nature of reality, the only things remaining are the positive emotions of generosity, compassion, tolerance, gentleness, courage, and wisdom. In this way, thought transformation is also how we "solve" the Third Condition of "ignorance" I mention in chapter 1.

Thus, we must confront our "enemy," our feelings of anger, fear, and desire, head on. We get hooked on these emotions. They are our habits, but they do not need to be. With thought transformation, we not only subdue these harmful emotions — harmful first to our own mental well-being, but also to the well-being of others — but we replace them and develop new habits that create a helpful, happier state of mind. The more we train, the better we get at this.

What is the true nature of reality that we are seeking? Much of the rest of this book is devoted to explaining and understanding this. Naturally, it's vital to know what one is aiming for in order to get the most out of mind training. For now, though, all we need to get started is a simple example that provides a basic understanding of how the mechanism works.

Let's say you have an appointment with your doctor. You show up on time, but the receptionist tells you that the doctor is running late. He's well over an hour behind schedule, probably two or three. The receptionist asks if you can come back later, or perhaps reschedule for another day.

How do you feel? Most of us would be irritated, if not angry. You have been inconvenienced through no fault of your own. You might think, if the doctor was that behind in his schedule, why couldn't the office have called to let you know, saving you the trip? If this has happened before with your doctor's office, maybe your emotional reaction is even stronger: How inept and arrogant are they, that they can't keep their appointments and treat their patients with common courtesy? Very soon, your blood pressure is sky high, and this resentment ruins the rest of your day.

This kind of event occurs seemingly every day in one form or another; we should expect it, rather than react with surprise. But by the time your emotions have ruined your peace of mind, it no longer matters what caused them. It does not really matter if the doctor and the office had a legitimate excuse or not. What's telling, in fact, is that if you learned the doctor had been called to the scene of a terrible bus accident and was at that moment saving the lives of dozens of children, you'd let your irritation go easily. In comparison with that situation, your inconvenience is next to nothing. But if you glimpsed the doctor sitting in the back, eating a sandwich and flirting with a nurse, you'd probably fly into a rage. The perceived injustice of your inconvenience would lead you to "blow up." The inconvenience is the same either way, but now you are actively and deliberately making it worse for yourself.

But we have a choice in how to react. Mind training helps us to stop, in the moment, and consider: Am I reacting out of blind emotional habit, and are my emotions appropriate and helpful? We notice any negative emotions and understand: Ah, I have a problem here. I cannot handle the disruption of injustice with equanimity. I am caught up in the drama I've created within my own mind. For the mind-training practitioner, this is an opportunity to employ those unique techniques found in transforming the emotions. As we do, the moment itself transforms: our main concern is no longer our inconvenience and its injustice, but learning from our reaction. The mind-training practitioner even experiences excitement or joy, or at least self-amusement, at the opportunity this problem has provided. Why? Because we know that the only way we can achieve the balanced state of mind of an awakened person is by confronting head on the habitual patterns that have imprisoned us for our entire life. If, in this moment, we can break one pattern now and forever, wouldn't we experience gratitude? It is in this way that we say we become "thankful" for our problems. This helps explain Lama Atisha's affection and appreciation for his cook. The mind-training practitioner thinks, "My old habits want to trap me and send me down a road that I will later regret. Instead, I'll use this situation as an opportunity to further develop my mind."

There is a rather strange and wonderful thing that happens with this kind of attitude: you become a happier person and people notice. Instead of always complaining, you begin to appreciate what life presents to you *and* use it to develop your mind. Mind training begins with practicing mindfulness and openness of the present moment. Then it takes what we observe through our present-moment awareness and transforms it into the positive qualities we seek to nurture and embody. All of the troubles we confront throughout our life are viewed as teachings. Of course, this practice does not come easily. We have to study and investigate so we have the right understandings — and then we have to practice and train so we become stronger and more skillful and can put them into practice whenever we need them, which is to say always. In this way, we create a happier and more balanced state of mind.

A JOURNEY IN FOUR STEPS

In developing our inner potential, we have to cultivate our awareness and mindfulness of what's going on inside of us. We take the lead in our well-being by being a student of the mind, of our own psychology. The beauty of the ancient approach to understanding our psychology and becoming healthy is that there are as many paths as there are people. Like traveling from San Francisco to New York, there are hundreds of routes. There are scenic routes and well-traveled routes, routes that are fast and routes that could take months. I think of the steps below as being an interstate with clear road signs and plenty of gas stations and restrooms on the journey.

Step One: You Have a Choice!

The first step we take in developing mental well-being, and employing mind training, is remembering that in every moment we choose how to direct our inner life. Most of us live our lives in reactive mode — we respond to things as they happen without considering our response. We are on automatic pilot. Lacking a sense of inner control, we typically respond by trying to control the world and others.

Step one is simply setting the intention to be aware. It is remembering to stop so you give yourself a choice in how to react. It is remembering that we are in control of our emotional life. It is the commitment to take responsibility for one's own inner reality. Our inner experience may be positive, it may be mundane, or it may be disturbing, but we are the only ones in control of it.

We have free will but only if we exercise it. We need to be utterly convinced that we can create something different for ourselves and that we have the potential to be our best and our happiest. Remembering that we are free is liberating in and of itself. Just remembering our potential to be free and in control eases the mind and brings a smile to our face.

Step Two: Set Up Your Laboratory

Once we foster present-moment awareness, we create a gap in our typical reactivity. This gap is empowering, but it is usually brief, and we must do something with it. We need to seize the opportunity to fill the gap with something different than our usual, habitual response.

This is where we begin to "recite" our ABCs. These ABCs were originally created by Rasmus Hougaard for the Potential Project, a corporate-based mindfulness training program, of which I am a senior trainer. I've adapted them for use here.

A: This stands for our anatomy. The first thing we do is check the state of our body:

1. First, see if you are holding tension anywhere, like in your chest, stomach, head, or jaw.
2. Then, relax the body, release the tension. If you can, sit down and make sure the spine is straight and head slightly bent. Take this as far as circumstances allow: take a break for a few minutes, gently close the eyes, and put your hands on your lap or knees. Relax.

B: This stands for breath. Bring your attention to your breath. It is your anchor. Don't breathe any differently; just connect and stay with it. Simply focus either on your belly rising and falling or the sensation at the nostrils. If you are feeling very agitated or distracted, it is better to focus on your belly. *Your breath is always your anchor throughout every exercise. You never lose focus on the breath.*

C: This stands for counting. After you connect with the breath, practice the "You Can Count on It" meditation in chapter 1. If this is a quick, on-the-run intervention, then count five exhalations in a row.

You have now set up your laboratory for learning and created a solid foundation to approach the problem.

Step Three: What's Going On?

In this step, you identify and name the emotion that is arising within your consciousness. This might be simple and obvious or more subtle. The emotion might be huge — a rage that overtakes you — or fairly mundane, an irritation that nettles. Your reaction might be complex, a mix of positive and negative emotions arising out of conflicting desires or a muddled confusion about the situation. In step three we connect with our inner world and identify what's going on. Without this knowledge, we can't take the next step and let go of or transform our emotions. We need this self-awareness to exercise our choice to become better and healthier human beings.

Chapter 4 discusses all of the "afflictive emotions" in detail. Turn there for a thorough understanding of these problematic states. A representative list would include: frustration, rage, resentment, impatience, self-loathing, annoyance, anxiety, fear, aversion, longing, competitiveness, jealousy, envy, a need for power or control, desire, doubt, and confusion.

Similarly, later chapters will also discuss the wholesome and positive emotions we are seeking to cultivate. Some are indeed treated like direct "opposites" of certain negative emotions, so that we counter (or transform) anger and blame with compassion and understanding, for instance. However, we can easily evaluate our success, even if we are still learning to identify our emotional states clearly, or are struggling to master the mind-training techniques: wholesome thoughts and emotions produce peace, harmony, and balance for oneself and others. They have an integrative effect upon one's own mind and even affect those around us. Other people, even animals, can sense a balanced, healthy mind. Whatever techniques or terms we use, if the result is a balanced and awakened mind, we are on the right track. On the contrary, if despite our efforts feelings of spite, anger, self-centeredness, or greed remain, then we still have work to do. The method is less important than the results.

Step Four: Take Action

Practicing the first three steps will calm the mind down and increase awareness. But if you really want to unseat the disturbing emotions as well as deepen your wisdom, then you need to take effective, positive action. Step four offers a number of interventions to try once you have connected with your inner experience using the first three steps. Which intervention you employ depends upon which techniques resonate for you and which technique is most effective with the particular emotion that is arising. As you begin, there may be an element of trial and error as you find what works best for you. However, the following techniques share a similar overall strategy.

The first goal is to understand and see the disturbing emotions as something external to your identity or sense of self. You create distance between the emotion and yourself. The emotion, thought, or feeling is "objectified" within your mind. By naming the emotion in step three, we begin to "externalize" the emotion, and in this step, we separate from it and end its influence over us. We can play with the emotion or feeling, hold it or let it go, or transform it in a variety of ways depending upon what we find helpful and what resonates with us.

One way to think of it is that we learn to "dance" with our emotions. They are like a dance partner with a particular attitude or point of view. We learn our own rhythms and how to shift tempos so that our dance is always beautiful. Another useful analogy is to regard the emotions as raw, like flour: our job is to create something edible out of them. We might convert our emotions into a variety of forms — a loaf of bread, a croissant, a doughnut, a wedding cake — each of them delicious. But if we leave them as raw flour, no one is nourished.

Now, sit with your breath. Sit with the emotion that is arising, and in your mind begin to surround, infuse, permeate, color, or envelop the emotion with one of the following practices. At first, these activities might feel intellectual and self-conscious, but with practice, they will become natural and reflexive and deepen with intuitive insights.

FLOAT LIKE A CLOUD IN THE SKY OF YOUR MIND

See how the emotion, thought, or feeling appears to be solid and unchanging. Now, shift your perspective to where you can actually see the emotion or thought within the clear sky of your mind. Like a cloud, it changes shape, blows across the sky, and eventually disappears. It loses its hold upon the mind. It arises, abides for a split second, and then fades away. As it gives way, another emotion, thought, or sensation arises, abides, and fades. This process may seem, at first, to take some time, perhaps a few minutes. As you get good you will see the constant flow of perceptions. A river, from afar, looks still; not until you get up close can you see that it is moving swiftly.

LET IT GO LIKE A FISH

Thoughts, emotions, and all mental experience are quite slippery. When you try to grasp and hold on to the inner experience, it slips away, like trying to grab a fish with one hand. Let it go, let it go, let it go. Problems arise, as we'll see, when we hold on to a moving object. Eventually your whole being will be in a relaxed state of letting go. This should be experiential, not intellectual.

BE HERE NOW

Another way we get into trouble is wanting things to be different than they are. Now, just *be* in the moment, moment to moment. When one is fully in the present moment, one is totally satisfied. Emotions and thoughts always tell us something different; they always encourage us to *do* something. Here, now, you are not a "human doing"; you are, for a few minutes, a "human being."

WHAT A BEAUTIFUL WORLD

Whatever is arising within your mind is your life in this moment. It's all you've got. This moment, not your past, is "who you are." Because what is arising in this moment is totally unique and new, it is extraordinary and beautiful. See yourself and the world around you without prejudice or judgment. Appreciate it for what it is. It is only our opinions, wants, desires, and assumptions that say, "This is bad. I don't like it, and I don't want it in my life." Or, "This is good. I like it, and I want more." In this strategy, it's all good because "It ain't nothin' till you make it somethin'."

YES, TEACHER

When we connect with ourselves inwardly, everything becomes our teacher. Whatever is arising within your mind you now approach with curiosity and courage. We ask of the experience, "What can you teach me?" We sit with the experience from a stance of curiosity and courage, openness and strength, and watch it, like a TV documentary, to see what we can learn from the experience we are having.

LET'S GO TO THE MOVIES

All of what goes on within our mindscape is merely image and language. Sit back and be entertained. Watch it all like a movie. However, with this movie you cannot get lost in the characters, dialogue, or story; just watch and enjoy, with the knowledge that you are just watching a movie. I used to tell my kids, when they were getting afraid during a scary movie, "Remember, it's just a movie with a bunch of actors, make-up, cameras, and props." Do the same when watching the movie playing within your mind. This method is especially effective when you find yourself obsessing about something. You can listen to the dialogue in your head like you are listening to a TV show or a radio play — but you are aware you are listening.

A BREATH OF FRESH AIR

This technique is very effective if you are feeling quite agitated, nervous, or unhappy, but it will work with any disturbing emotion. Remember, throughout all of the techniques you are never losing the focus on the breath, even if it becomes less predominant. Now, you are going to use the breath actively: as you exhale naturally through your nostrils, see the negative emotion you are experiencing as a dark, gray, toxic cloud that is expelled, fading to the far corners of the world and dissolving. Then, as you naturally inhale, breathe in light and radiant color, and all the positive emotions like contentment, joy, ease, and bliss. Do not control the breath; just use it for your visualization.

I OBJECT!

This technique does not follow the same protocol as the ones above. It is not a separate step but merely another option. This technique requires a little mental gymnastics. After you have named the emotion, thought, sensation, or experience that is arising, quickly switch perspective. Look at, and focus upon, the subject of the experience — yourself. Ask, "Who is sad? Who is angry? Who is it that is experiencing this experience?" Now, after zeroing in on that self, let it go, let it fade or drift away, in the same way you let emotions and perceptions go in the other methods. The goal of this technique is to see our sense of self, or individual identity, as fluid and changing, not solid, static, and permanent. As we will see later, we accumulate an identity that we come to regard as immutable, but this self is not real in the sense that it does not actually exist the way we think it does. In other words, if you can let go of the self that always feels anger, then you let go of the anger. When you get good at this, all of your problems, struggles, and difficulties will soften and loosen their grip upon you.

THE POWER OF ENTHUSIASM

In the beginning of mind training, one of the most important positive emotions to cultivate is enthusiasm. It is easy to become discouraged or to feel overwhelmed. Consider: How many times each day do you become angry? Three, five, twelve, more? To be honest, if we stopped to address and transform every negative emotion each time one occurred, we'd probably never get anything done. Particularly in the beginning, this focus on engaging problems can seem to make one's life appear worse, as we notice just how buffeted by disturbing emotions we usually are. Until we become more adept at mind training, we may feel we are not up to the daunting task it asks of us.

In Buddhist psychology, depression, self-pity, and laziness are countered and transformed by enthusiasm. So, early on, if you have to pick your battles, do battle with self-pity. My teacher Lama Yeshe used to say that, from his dealings with Western people, he felt one of our primary obstacles is our tendency to feel sorry for ourselves. Self-pity is a totally nonproductive state of mind and thoroughly self-indulgent; nobody likes hanging around a self-pitying person, including ourselves. The more we indulge in self-pity, the more unhappy we become. For many people, self-pity becomes such a way of being that they become habitually depressed, and yet they often do not remember why. Naturally, there are always reasons — they may have broken up with a partner, lost someone they loved, been reprimanded at work, or lost their job. If, as we practice mind training, we start to feel we are always failing and "just can't do it," recognize this as self-pity, which does absolutely nothing to rectify the situation. When you recognize this disturbing emotion, stop and practice the four steps. Then transform this "problem" with enthusiasm. Let go of the voice inside that pushes help away, saying, "Leave me alone. I'd rather feel bad. If you were me, you'd feel the same way."

Remember, attitude is the major factor in all mental health and happiness. Without enthusiasm, no approach will work. When you feel self-pity, consider the life of Nick Vujicic. Nick is happy despite having been born without arms and legs. He often says, "I love living life. I'm happy!" Nick is a motivational speaker who gives talks to schoolchildren, prisoners, business leaders, and others. Check out one of his videos on the Internet; he'll probably make you cry. His motto: "No arms, no legs, no worries."

Nick is an example of the transformative power of enthusiasm, the willingness to tackle any and every problem, no matter what it is. My teacher Lama Yeshe was another such example. He was truly a phenomenal man. Like others who have cultivated a deep level of mental health, he naturally drew people to him. Whether Lama Yeshe was teaching or casually interacting with others, you felt like you could not get enough. He was never boring, and yet he was not engaging just to be noticed or to feel important. He just had an unending interest in other people and in the world at large. He was curious. He was a learner. He was 100 percent open and was never defensive. And yet, he was no pushover. He had strong convictions about what was right and what was wrong, and while he enjoyed all that life could offer, he was disciplined and adhered strictly to his monk's code of conduct. Most telling of all, people felt good around Lama Yeshe. He was an environment all by himself. Time and again people would recognize that when they were with Lama Yeshe they could catch glimpses of their higher potential. People would feel, "I really can attain awakening. It is not some fantasy but an actual, real state of mind that any of us can achieve." Because Lama Yeshe did not have a personal agenda, an ego to feed, prop up, or nurture, he was a microclimate that allowed a person to experience themselves in a way that was liberating and uncrowded. One felt that anything was possible. Lama used to say, "People think I do magic. They think I do some sort of miracles or magic with their minds. But I tell you: it is not me who is magic. It is the mind that is magic!"

Enthusiasm is infectious; others are encouraged by it. With enthusiasm, we view our problems as opportunities to build our character and our inner potential. It is that simple. Events can be seen either as threatening, out to destroy us, or as prospects to awaken our deepest and most wholesome qualities. Either we can continue to allow events to give rise to our defensive reactions or we can open our hearts and minds to a deeper appreciation of the world, the people around us, and ourselves.

With the four steps of mind training, we start a new relationship with ourselves. We commit to kicking the bad habit of reacting to our disturbing emotions. What is this like in practice? Let's say you have an argument with your friend Jason. Afterward you say to yourself: "Jason really got me angry, so I'm going to tell him off the next time I see him." With step one, you instantly recognize your anger and make a choice: first you will resolve your anger, and once that's done, you'll decide how to respond to whatever Jason did or said. So, you set your intention. Then, in step two, you focus your mind by using your breath. You calm down so you can regard the emotions you're feeling with objectivity. You don't deny the anger, or tell yourself you shouldn't feel that way, or try to justify your angry reaction. You just calm down so that you can look at your anger as if it were a strange object you could hold in your hand. In step three, you regard your anger closely, as if you are examining a painting for the first time. Aren't the colors interesting? What kind of anger is it: of shame, injustice, hurt? Is this anger big or small, loud or soft?

In step four, you do something with it. Perhaps you see your anger as a cloud in a blue sky. You watch the cloud: it is changeable, fluid, impermanent. Keep watching the emotion change shape until it dissipates or is blown away in the breeze. Notice the anger arising, abiding, and then slipping into nothingness.

Or perhaps, when you recognize your anger, turn to it as if it were your teacher, your very own rude chef, and ask, "What is it you're here to teach me? I'm a student now. I want to learn." Don't feel shame over your anger; ask it to teach you, then listen to what it says.

Or, simply breathe. As in "A Breath of Fresh Air," just breathe out the anger, and breathe in compassion and empathy. Keep breathing in this way until all the anger is expelled and only compassion remains. As we will see later, feeling compassion isn't done to justify or excuse the hurtful actions of others, but to move ourselves beyond moralistic judgment.

Or, turn the tables on yourself: as in "I Object!" redirect your focus. Ignore the anger and focus on the particular "self" that's angry, the "I" in "I am angry." What narrative is justifying this self's existence? Indeed, where is the "I"? Can you soften your ego, and give the anger no "self" to cling to?

Our primary focus in mind training is to first resolve the conflict within ourself. When that is done, resolving the conflict with Jason comes next. However, what's also true is that once we resolve the conflict within ourselves, our conflicts with others often shrink to small size or even disappear entirely. Not coincidentally, Jason also probably benefits from our mind training.

Thus, just by enthusiastically embracing our "problems," and seeing our negative emotions as tools for self-awareness, we effect positive change and help others. Enthusiasm itself demonstrates our commitment to our inner development and to being a force for healing in our relationships. We know our happiness is not going to be derived from the outer world, but from inner change, and so we make the decision to solve our own problems, rather than blame or curse others. We know we have the inner potential to be healthier, happier, and more balanced human beings. We take our well-being into our own hands.

Our enthusiasm also says, while we know that we must understand ourselves completely, the good and the bad, we are doing so out of kindness, for ourselves and for others. We are developing the ability to become familiar with ourselves from a nonshaming perspective so that we may embody our best selves. This naturally benefits everyone, as it makes us more loving, kind, and caring. With enthusiasm, we loosen our judgment and sharpen our discernment. We distinguish between what is helpful and healthy versus what is unhelpful and disturbing. This discernment makes us wiser human beings and more pleasant to be around.

We also know that this discernment makes us more skillful. We can more easily employ methods and techniques to eliminate, confront, avert, and transform the negative, hurtful emotions and cultivate and nurture the healthy ones. And we know that as we become more skilled in mind training, we become stronger, too. We know we will be able to quiet our mind more readily, and observe it with increased detachment, even curiosity, no matter what emotional storms blow through. We become students of our mind and of the world, observing and studying all with detached engagement. In this way we become true scientists engaged in the pure pursuit of discovery. We see our inner world like an artist observing a seascape before she has applied color to canvas, or an athlete who is "in the zone"; we gain a sense of pure being beyond language. In remaining detached from the chatter of the mind, we come to embody pure peace, contentment, and happiness.

Most important of all, these feelings are not just ours alone. While mind training is work we do on ourselves, it is driven by the desire to help and be of benefit to others. Our enthusiasm is not self-centered but forms the basis of a more compassionate approach to life and our relationships. Ultimately, as we will see in the final chapter, we are most successful in alleviating our own suffering when our efforts are dedicated with enthusiasm and compassion to alleviating the suffering of all others. We are inspired by the belief that as we create a new, healthier world for ourselves, we create a healthier world for everyone.

BLESSINGS

Along with enthusiasm, gratitude is another essential attitude, and it's one that mind training cultivates. Gratitude says: If good things happen, we're thankful. If bad things happen, we're thankful. All life is a blessing, and anything that happens can be used to feed our inner development and happiness.

Here is one of my favorite stories about gratitude. In the early 1980s, in the middle of my time in Nepal, I attended a two-week retreat at a hermitage in the Himalayas, which was attended by a couple dozen Western students and several local sherpas. For some years leading up to this time, the Kingdom of Nepal had begun experimenting with democracy, adopting a political system that was a kind of democratic monarchy based loosely on the British model. However, in actuality, the royal family ran the country as a nepotistic theocracy. The king was regarded as an incarnation of a Hindu god. Corruption was a way of life and a way of governance. While there was a parliament, the local populace did not have a hand in electing their representatives. But the king was slowly loosening up the tight grip of the monarchy, and during this period the king decided to hold local elections, which were to take place during the middle of the retreat. One of my primary teachers, Lama Zopa Rinpoche, was eager to participate in this historic election, and when the time came, he asked me to accompany him to the place where he had to vote, the village of his birthplace, itself high in the Himalayas.

The hermitage, called Lawudo, is extremely remote, at an altitude of thirteen thousand feet, and it was established by Lama Zopa many years earlier. In fact, this hermitage is built next to a cave where a great meditator, considered the previous incarnation of Lama Zopa, meditated for over thirty years. Still today, there are no roads, running water, sewage, or telephones; then there was no electricity either. To reach Lawudo, one either walks for nine days from the nearest road or flies in and walks another two days. It is stunningly beautiful and rugged.

Lama Zopa Rinpoche's birthplace, a small village named Thame, is in the Solu Khumbu region of Nepal. Thame is in a remote valley at an altitude of about eleven thousand feet, and it is a hardy hour and a half walk through the mountains from Lawudo. On the day of the vote, Rinpoche and I left in the late morning and arrived in Thame just after noon. However, Rinpoche was a well-known figure in the region, and his arrival in the small village was a big deal. Upon arrival, we were continually stalled by local farmers and herders asking him to have tea in their homes, bless their children, or perform a healing rite for someone who was sick. Rinpoche did not want to deny anyone, but if I wasn't vigilant about the time, it could be hours before we reached the polling station, which might close.

After several short delays, we were almost at the polling station when Rinpoche was approached by a distant relative in great distress. Someone close to him had just died. The family and relatives were just beginning the very important ceremonies that need to be done to ensure safe passage and a good rebirth for the deceased. While there were local lamas preparing to perform the necessary rites, having an esteemed master like Lama Zopa Rinpoche at the ceremony would be extraordinarily auspicious for the descendent and extremely comforting for the family. Rinpoche immediately agreed to attend the ceremony.

I was in a quandary. The ceremony normally takes several hours, and I silently fretted about the polling station closing and Rinpoche missing the rare opportunity to vote. Finally, I spoke my concerns, yet Rinpoche seemed detached and unmoved by my urging that he first cast his vote and then attend the ceremony. However, he eventually gave in to my plan, and we tried to walk quickly through the village to the polling station despite being constantly delayed by the many adoring villagers, who were delighted at having their local son and renowned lama in their midst.

When we arrived at the polling station, there was a line of voters still waiting. Voting officials sat behind a rickety wood desk out in the open air. On their desks were large notebooks of lined rice paper with each citizen's handwritten name. As each person approached, the officials searched out the voter's name and checked it off, and then the person went behind a curtain to vote. When Rinpoche reached the desk, the official maintained a professional air while searching for Lama Zopa's name in the registry. The official certainly did not want to disappoint the notable voter who had shown up in his small outpost. But, alas, after much searching, Lama Zopa's name was nowhere to be found. There was no explanation or other recourse. Lama Zopa was prohibited from voting.

Unmoved, Rinpoche quickly found his way back to his relative's house to perform the rites for the person who had passed away. The ceremony took several hours, and I then became concerned that we would have to trek back to Lawudo in the dark. By late afternoon, we finally started the arduous ninety-minute walk to the hermitage. As we were nearing Lawudo, and most of the daylight had disappeared, Rinpoche turned to me and said, "I'm so happy I went to vote. I'm sure the reason I went was not to vote but to be able to offer some benefit to the family who had lost their loved one."

Rinpoche demonstrated several things to me that day. One is, if we drop our attachments to what we desire, we will not be overwhelmed by disturbing emotions and can see the benefit in any apparent upset or problem. Despite the extraordinary effort voting involved, and the historic importance of the election itself, Rinpoche's mind never moved. His attitude never wavered. In fact, by day's end, he was as elated as he'd been when we started out.

Everything remained good. His mind remained happy. He wasn't consoling himself that a bad event had been "saved" by a good one; he was simply expressing gratefulness for everything that had happened. This is the true practice of mind training, of transforming the emotions. With this practice, we see things differently. For as Rinpoche demonstrated, things don't exist as they appear.

CHAPTER THREE

What Was I Thinking?

"The human mind has both positive and negative sides. But the negative is transient, very temporary. Your up and down emotions are like clouds in the sky; beyond them, the real, basic human nature is clear and pure."

—— LAMA THUBTEN YESHE

When His Holiness the Dalai Lama was still a teenager and isolated within his palace in his Himalayan kingdom of Tibet, he was kept from venturing out freely into the city; thus, he began working on some old cars that had been given to his predecessor. In those days there were virtually no automobiles in Tibet. The Dalai Lama, through curiosity and trial and error, carefully tinkering for hours, learned how an engine worked until he was able to make the cars drivable. Prior to restoring the automobiles, not only did he know nothing about cars or engines, there was almost no one in the country he could ask for advice aside from the occasional foreign diplomat.

Like the Dalai Lama learning how an engine worked, we should take a beginner's approach to learning about our mind. Thus, we become both the scientist and the test subject, while our life experiences become our inner laboratory. This chapter addresses the most basic and essential question: What is the true nature of mind?

Buddhism proposes an essential distinction: humans, in fact all living beings, possess minds that are pure, clear, and luminous. This clarity is something we are born with, and it is the same for everyone. Then there are our thoughts, emotions, feelings, cogitations, images, fantasies, perceptions, and so on. In common usage, we in the modern world typically refer to all this "mental stuff" as just "thoughts," and for ease of reference (unless I state otherwise) I use the word "thoughts" to include all of this mental activity. However, note that in Buddhist psychology it is too limiting to simply use the word "thoughts" to refer to all of the mental realm, and so I use the word cautiously and with the most expansive understanding. There are many parts, or functions, of the mind, just like there are many employees and departments functioning in a company. One part of the mind can perceive another part of the mind, and thus, we perceive and relate through our thoughts, emotions, feelings, and so on.

Our luminous mind along with our thoughts, emotions, and feelings constitute our mental activity, and these are ephemeral, changeable, and not solidly existing. Take the impressions of our senses. Our eyes see and our hands feel, and we label these sensations: rock, breeze, tree. But when we experience "rock," so much of our experience is a mental fabrication: the colors are seen by our mind, its shape is conceived by our mind, its hardness is registered within our mind. The rock has no independent reality. The rock's very existence is dependent upon our mind perceiving it. To put it another way, the world exists, just not the way it appears to us. The world appears to exist independently of what we perceive in our heads when, in fact, our experience of the world depends upon what we see and experience inside of ourselves.

Further, we interpret and evaluate: This rock is good, that rock is bad. I like a summer breeze, but not a wintry blast. Experience, in a sense, is neutral, but the range of our mental activity includes all kinds of judgments and emotions — agitation, anger, longing, arrogance, confusion, jealousy, competitiveness, sadness, and so on. We develop preferences, and this becomes our personality, and soon we are fooled: we come to believe our thoughts really are the way they appear, and our individual self really exists the way it appears, so that what is "real" is whatever we have come to believe it to be. Our thoughts embellish the raw data of our senses and thus distort the true nature of ourselves and reality. When we are thus confused (or suffering the Third Condition of ignorance), the emotions have free rein and disturb our natural balance. They rob us of our peace, contentment, and mental well-being. *And that's where our problems begin.*

One simple, classic Buddhist analogy is to regard our mind like a mirror. The mind is clear, and it reflects whatever a person experiences. These images, thoughts, and feelings do not affect the mirror. The mirror is indifferent whether it reflects a beautiful sunset or a muddy road. Additionally, the reflections in the mirror change from moment to moment. Likewise, what appears in our mind constantly shifts and varies, arises and disappears.

Another common metaphor Buddhist scholars use for the mind is the sky. The sky is itself clear, but within it can appear storm clouds, smog, fog, high wispy clouds, rain, snow, and sleet. The sky appears to change colors from blue to gray to black. And yet, these colors are not the actual sky itself, which like space is colorless. The actual nature of the sky, or space, does not change depending upon what is happening within it. Still, experiences or events do occur, and they are constantly changing from moment to moment. So it is in our mind, where we have an ever-changing weather pattern of emotions and experiences — some stormy, some light and airy, some foggy and dense, and some mundane and ordinary. The sky of our mind holds the subject of our experience, but its nature is clean and pure.

THE THREE UMPIRES:
REALITY IS WHAT WE LABEL IT

Three umpires are sitting in a bar, sharing a beer together. They begin talking about their job and the difficulties they face in calling balls and strikes. The first umpire states quite confidently, "There's balls and there's strikes, and I call them as they are!" The second umpire, with a slight look of disapproval, says, "No, no, no, there's balls and there's strikes, and I call them as I see 'em." The third umpire says, "You know, you're both wrong. There's balls and there's strikes, and they ain't nothin' till I call 'em."

And like that, nothing exists until we perceive, label, and interpret it.

Or, put differently: The first umpire claims we perceive the world as it actually exists. The second umpire claims we interpret the world that exists. The third claims we create the world through our perception of it.

Every single moment of our life we are experiencing something, even if we are not aware of what we are experiencing. Even while we are unconscious or asleep, there is still perception. Neuroscientists now believe that within our brains there are over 11 million neurons firing each second! The firing of these neurons occurs when the brain is active and having some kind of experience. Thus, there is always something filtering through our mind.

Raw experience, though, almost never remains in that form. Once it rises to a conscious thought, we have already labeled and interpreted it. The colors and movement have become a baseball, and we've further judged whether it's a ball or a strike, good or bad. It may seem like we are passive perceivers, but we are actually

active engagers, though we are usually unaware that we are constantly interpreting, creating reality as it happens. This engagement
happens automatically and seemingly out of our control, moment to
moment. And it's true, we can't stop our thoughts. The only reality
we know is our concept of it. Life is nothing till we call it something,
and this is where mind training comes in. Through it, we learn to
hold our concepts loosely, particularly those that allow unhelpful
emotions to take over and cause us problems.

Disturbing emotions are so called because they hypnotize us,
in effect, so they become "reality." These particular thoughts cloud
the clarity of mind so that it is completely obscured, and we act as
if what exists in our mind is real, unchanging, immutable. We live
our life constantly jumping from emotion to emotion, fearing and
cursing the balls and strikes coming our way, and forget that we are
the ones who created balls and strikes. To create a meaningful, self-
directed life, we must confront the untamed, undisciplined, uncon-
trolled mental activity that we have let run us.

To take an everyday example, consider drinking a latte. Initially,
we drink coffee because we are thirsty; we enjoy the taste and smell,
and we like how the caffeine gives us a boost. But eventually, our
happiness depends on coffee. We feel we can't start a day without
it, and even more, we aren't truly happy unless we've had "good"
coffee, our favorite latte. And we no longer just drink our favorite
latte; we evaluate each one critically, judging it too hot or too cold,
too strong or too weak, too bland or too sweet, and so on. We become unhappy if we have anything that falls short of a "perfect"
latte. Suddenly, every morning revolves around our "need" for coffee and our "desire" for the best, and our entire emotional self might
hang in the balance. This is crazy. Sadly, we live much of our life at
the mercy of such fantasies, and is it a wonder that lasting peace and
satisfaction are elusive?

IN SEARCH OF THE MIND

In my formal training as a psychotherapist I was never given a definition of "mind." If we are to be called a psychotherapist, a person who heals the mind, it is unconscionable to not have a definition of mind. Dr. Daniel Siegel, a psychiatrist and leading researcher of neuroscience, has claimed that he has asked over eighty-five thousand mental health professionals if they had received formal instruction on the nature of the mind, and if they had a coherent working definition of mind. He has stated that less than 3 percent of the mental health professionals respond positively to the question.

From one point of view, this confusion as to the nature of mind is rather shocking. We have had this mind since the day of our birth. We refer to our mind constantly. When we say, "I feel sad today," or "I'm happy to see you," or "I love rocky road ice cream," we are referring to states of mind or experiences we have within us. But where are those emotions and opinions? They are nonphysical parts of ourselves that seem to dwell within. But if we can't properly locate and define our emotions and thoughts, then can we even properly define our own self, the "I" or "me" that has opinions? Our mind is constantly chattering within us: "I need a cup of coffee. I need to sit down. I need to go to work. I want to call my son." Ad infinitum.

Hence, we can point to our bodies and say we have an entire universe inside of us, but there is no physical manifestation of our consciousness. So, who is this person we relate to as "me" who has all of these feelings and thoughts and attitudes and emotions and dreams and fantasies and longings and fears and worries and frustrations? I mean, *where in the world, where in our being, are all these events going on?*

We might say, "In the brain." But examine the physical organ of the brain, and we cannot find the actual thoughts. And in any case, the brain depends on the five senses for information to know anything: so, in actuality our experience extends beyond the brain to our fingers, ears, eyes, skin, and tongue. It appears that the mind, which is formless, extends to all parts of our body, but the brain surely does not. Let's say we're eating a nice bowl of rocky road ice cream: What of this experience is inherently in the bowl, what is in our tongue, and what is only in our mind? The bowl is full of potential sensations that the mind conjures into "chocolate" and "cold" and "delicious." Thus, whatever is in the bowl that our tongue encounters, our personal experience of rocky road ice cream exists primarily within our mind. It almost seems like a crime that we don't really know where the "chocolate" is, where "happiness" resides, how they arise and how they disappear and where they go. Despite everything we "know" about the world, we know so little about the very thing doing the knowing, the creator and constant companion to our every experience — our mind.

Perhaps the best we can do, for now, is acknowledge the simplest distinction, and this is the approach of Buddhist psychology. A living being is nothing more than two components: *a form or body* and *a mind*. The mind is nonatomic and nonmaterial, and so it cannot be seen, heard, smelled, felt, or tasted. It includes our emotions, feelings, thoughts, fantasies, dreams, musings, moods, and so on, both conscious and unconscious. We have plenty of conscious thoughts, and these typically constitute what we think of as our "self," but there are numerous unconscious impressions and evaluations that go on below our awareness, and these are equally "in the mind," though we don't direct or control them. Our senses constantly create these imprints, and we become consciously aware only of some. One way to characterize "the mind" would be to say that "the mind is the subject of any experience." In this sense, when we say, "I see the house," we understand that there is a physical object being observed by some entity, but the specific concepts of yourself, your observation, and "house" are subjective. They are only in the mind.

Another quality of the mind is that it is utterly fluid. It is not a static, unchanging, or fixed entity. By definition, it is formless. We observe how easily our thoughts and opinions can shift, sometimes on a dime, and even the "truth" of our five senses changes moment to moment. As our physical experiences of the world shift constantly, so our interpretation and concepts of the world are in a constant state of change. This quality of fluidity, of change, is one of our greatest allies. Were the mind truly fixed like concrete — and admittedly, it certainly feels that way when we are stuck in a depressive mood — then there would be no way out. It is the mind's very nature of pliability and flexibility that allows us to fully transform unwanted experiences. Further, as we discover the mind's nature of clarity, its ability to reflect our thoughts accurately while remaining unaffected, we can take great hope that we can develop skills of thought transformation that we have never possessed before.

But it's also important to remember that the physical world is not static either. Everything in the physical world is in constant flux, being born, getting older, dying, dissolving. Each day, our own bodies are older and a little different. This fluidity in the physical world extends to our own brains, the "organ of thought." Recent discoveries show how the brain is not fixed but has plasticity, and that the brain can actually be rewired. Mind training makes sense in this context as well: it is a way of changing and rewiring our neuro-pathways. Even if certain ways of thinking are "hardwired" into the physical brain, we can change our neuro-pathways and undo patterns we developed throughout our life and create new mental habits. In this way, at least, it's true that as we change our thoughts through a process of mental development, we change the physical world, the shape of our brain. But remember: The mind is not synonymous with the brain. They are not the same entity. However, they are interdependent. Simply speaking, the brain can be called the organ of the mind just like the eye is the organ of sight. The brain influences the mind and the mind can influence the brain, and all is fluid in a mysterious dance.

I AM LIKE A CAMERA: IMPRINTS AND PROJECTIONS

One of the most significant, perhaps unique, aspects of Buddhist psychology is the idea concerning imprints. As I said above, there is never a moment, whether we are aware of it or not, when the mind is not active. That means there is a subject — "you" — engaged in an experience. These "experiences" can be apparent or they can be exceedingly subtle. For example, as you read this book, you are aware of the words and their meaning. You are thinking, evaluating, and reacting emotionally as you read, shifting between engagement or distraction, enjoyment or boredom, confusion or comprehension. That is the gross experience of reading this book. Then, you are also registering various more subtle experiences as you are reading: the sensation of the book being held by your hands, the lawn mower off in the distance, the colors and lighting surrounding you. Furthermore, some of these impressions are so subtle they would be considered "unconscious": background thoughts and feelings, the rhythm of your heart beating, the air touching every pore of your body, and the faint sounds that touch your ears. Certain experiences remain outside of our usual state of awareness, and we have no conscious experience of these events. Even when we are asleep, there is experience. Even when we are in a coma, the brain remains active.

A useful way to think of this is that the mind is like a video camera and a TV screen rolled into one and working simultaneously. Our senses and our mind are like a video camera that is constantly recording, and every object we experience leaves a mental imprint. We may not be conscious of every imprint, but each is there, similar to the way whatever enters the lens of the camera becomes imprinted on the film or disc. For instance, if we were filming our daughter playing soccer, we'd be focused on her: we'd zoom in on her kicking a goal and celebrating afterward. That's what we are consciously focused on. But nonetheless and at the same time we are recording everything that comes in view of the lens: the players around her, the color of the grass, the traffic going by on a side street, and so on. It is like the mind has six lenses recording at the same time — the traditional five senses plus the mind itself — and these six "senses" are picking up a lot of imprints that we are not aware of. In fact, we are probably only aware of an infinitesimal amount of the actual imprints generated by our senses. Just think of all of the possible sensory and mental experiences that have happened just since you sat down to read. Next, think about how that is happening every minute throughout your day, every day throughout your life. That's a lot of experiences. That's a lot of filming. That's a lot of imprints. Sometimes I refer to this as our mental DNA.

Now, what's even more intriguing is that not only are we constantly filming, laying imprints upon our consciousness, but we are also projecting our experience as well. We are both a film camera and a film projector at the same time. Almost instantly, in our minds, we take the raw data of experience and interpret it, and then project our understanding onto the world (which includes ourselves). We do not live in bare experience. We live in a world of interpretation, assumption, and projection. We wear tinted glasses.

Because we constantly and immediately superimpose our interpretation upon experience, we never really experience things as they are. We experience things as *we are*. Everything we experience, *everything*, is experienced with our biases added to it immediately in the very next moment. This projection is how we create our own story, our own sense of self. Through our projections, the world, then, comes to reflect who we believe we are back to us, reinforcing the notion that we "know" the world when we really are seeing our own creation. We superimpose our likes and dislikes, we confirm our assumptions, and we react from our past experiences. We call things balls and strikes, and by doing so, we become umpires. Conversely, if we decide that our "true nature" is an umpire, then we are duty bound to treat the world like a game of baseball. We might say: sports are entertaining, French fries are delicious, and littering is bad, and these are just our personal balls and strikes. The stronger we become attached to these beliefs and previous imprints, the more we tend to reinforce them, interpreting each new object of experience (whether a thought, feeling, or physical sensation) so it fits our "story." Of course, we can change our habitual patterns. However solid our self seems, we can revise our personal movie anytime. That is one of the beauties and gifts of being human, but it takes great effort and intention. If we operate in our usual mode of automatic pilot, nothing will change, and we will continue to reinforce and even strengthen our habitual patterns and negative conditioning.

Another everyday story helps show this in action. Some time ago, my family and I were traveling to Australia to spend Christmas with my wife's family. My wife, two of my three children, and I were flying into Los Angeles. Our oldest child was flying from Colorado and was going to connect with us in LA. Our son had a three-hour layover in LA — plenty of time to make the connection with us and our fifteen-hour nonstop flight to Australia. However, that day it was stormy throughout the United States, and it was a few days before Christmas. Airports were chaotic and all flights were booked to capacity. Our son's flight was delayed leaving Denver.

An hour before we were to board our flight in LA, our son's plane still hadn't landed, and we started to worry. Finally, twenty minutes before our scheduled departure, the Denver flight arrived, but now our worry only got worse. We started to panic. There was no physical way our son could get his bags and reach our terminal, a quarter mile away, in time, and airline personnel said that if he missed the flight, he wouldn't get on another one for several days.

His entire trip and our Australia plans were in jeopardy. We pleaded with the airline staff to wait, to send a cart to get him, to let security know that he'd be coming and racing to get the flight. With fifteen minutes until takeoff, our son still hadn't even retrieved his bags, and staff told us it was totally hopeless.

What's interesting is that each person who was involved had the same raw data, what could be called the objective "facts": inclement weather, delayed flights, booked-to-capacity planes, and rigid airline schedules. But not only did most react with a range of almost-predictable disturbing emotions, we created narratives that projected what we expected to happen. I created a panicked drama of frustration and total powerlessness. All I saw were airline staff unwilling to bend the rules or help, and that's what I encountered. I feared our trip was turning into a disaster, and so I found no relief from my suffocating anxiety. Everyone I encountered was, I grumbled angrily, a "selfish, insensitive drone" causing me to enter my own little realm of hell.

Meanwhile, with similar data, my wife stayed fairly calm. She didn't despair or become enraged, and she kept talking to various staff, seeking for a solution. Finally, like a miracle, she found a supervisor who agreed to intervene, and at the same time, our LA plane was delayed for two hours, until our son was able to make the flight. The supervisor, with the same data, clearly created a different narrative than the other airline staff: it was indeed possible to hold a flight for the benefit of a few late passengers. The supervisor was very balanced, and when I apologized for taking her away from her job, she responded, "That's okay. You are my job." What I wonder, and what we can't know for sure, is whether the supervisor would have done the same thing if I, not my wife, had spoken to her first. My "story" was that no one would or could help us, and my wife's "story" was that someone might, and we each experienced events so that they confirmed our narratives.

What does all of this mean? It means that based upon our history, our temperament, our patterns in how we look at things, there could arise multiple emotions and attitudes around a single event. I was distraught, and my anxiety was 100 percent unhelpful. It was a disturbing emotion at full maturity. In reality, this emotion was merely an "object" in my mind, like the plane and the airline schedule and my son. And I fit it into a narrative: I "justified" my anxiety by creating a story to support it. No one could talk me out of my anxiety because there was no way, I believed, to avoid this obvious, almost-predictable disaster story (I mean, look at the facts!). Some parents sitting near us reassured us not to worry. They didn't care if we were delayed as long as our son made the flight, while other passengers were annoyed and getting agitated at the inconvenience our unexpected good fortune was causing them. And so it goes.

This event was such an astonishing lesson in how we create our own reality and how we have so little control over our minds if we don't seize the moment. If we can catch ourselves losing it, then we can create a different, healthier experience for ourselves and those around us. We can transform our mind, and thus our world, into one in which we prefer to live.

WHO NEEDS SLEEP?

In my airport story, it's relatively easy to imagine using the four steps of mind training successfully — once I noticed my anxiety, I could have stopped, calmed my mind by focusing on my breath, identified my emotions (and my "story"), and transformed them into a positive alternative. Though it didn't feel like it in the moment, my problem wasn't truly serious, and my emotional experience was clearly of my own making. But is it really true that *all thoughts* are only objects in the mind that can be released and transformed? It is true, and a couple of extraordinary stories of the incredible potential of mind training make this clear.

I remember when I was seventeen and just beginning to look at my inner world. I had become disenchanted with the whole drug scene. I was looking for insight and answers, and it seemed that my experiences with marijuana and psychedelics no longer offered me new answers. This was in the late sixties, at the dawning of the New Age movement, and I was interested in this whole new spiritual movement being imported from the East. The Beatles were playing sitars and making trips to India. Woodstock was inaugurated by an Indian guru, and people were shaving their heads and leaving a little tuft on top, dressing in pink, and chanting weird songs on street corners. I was curious and began to investigate.

I gravitated toward yoga at one of the more up-and-coming yoga centers in Los Angeles. The founder was Swami Satchidananda, the same swami who had opened the Woodstock Festival. One day at the center about seventy-five people were invited to attend a private talk by Swami Satchidananda. I remember being thoroughly struck by his presence. He was very peaceful yet commanding. He seemed kind and had a sense of humor. His illuminating lecture lasted about an hour, and when he finished, he glided out of the room just as he had glided in. He seemed to walk without disturbing the air around him.

Later that day, a friend of mine who was attending the same event remarked how impressed he was with Satchidananda's mental attainments, achieved through meditation. I was curious how he would know another person's inner achievements. My friend remarked, "Well, he must have developed some sort of mental power. Swami didn't tell us, but when he was walking into the lecture, he stepped on a two-inch sewing needle. He gave his whole talk, walked out, and spoke with a number of people before he was alone in his room before lunch. At that point, he asked me if I could pull it out for him, since he couldn't get a good grip on it. He never once gave any indication of pain or discomfort."

If the mind can let go of and remain unaffected by the experience of physical pain, then surely it can subdue and transform the "pain" of any disturbing emotion. Even physical pain, once we become conscious of it, is just a thought, an object we can control in the mind. Not only that, but we can gain control over aspects of our physical self that seem automatic and essential, like hunger and sleep.

Up until the last several years (after contracting diabetes), one of my close teachers, Lama Zopa Rinpoche, had not slept for more than an hour or so at a time in the thirty-five years I had known him. I believe that scientists will say that it is humanly impossible to function on such little sleep. In the instance of my teacher, Lama Zopa developed a very advanced level of meditation when he was a young man. Among the Buddhist and Hindu contemplative traditions, it is well known that through meditative practices the need for sleep is replaced with deep and sustained concentration. I have spent many nights with Rinpoche, working on different projects, engaging in various ceremonies, and at one point I was living in the same room with him for several weeks. I never once saw him lie down or sleep. It's true, I wasn't with him every single moment, and I've seen how in deep sitting meditation his chin will fall to his chest for a few minutes. But this is also a typical result of someone in deep meditation. However, there's no denying that Lama Zopa has learned to control his need for sleep to a degree far beyond a normal person.

Lama Zopa has accomplished many unusual and seemingly impossible feats like this. At an earlier age, he stopped eating food altogether. He did not experience any hunger pains or anguish when he was not eating. He ate nothing for several days. Admittedly, the body can go without food for some weeks, but the person will generally be suffering and in distress. In Lama Zopa's case there was no sense of angst, pain, or worry. In fact, in place of suffering, he seemed to be more and more happy and at ease. However, he did become progressively thinner, and it seemed he would just "evaporate" if he did not start eating. People around him began pleading with him to eat, but he didn't until Rinpoche's own teacher commanded him to take sustenance because, as the teacher stated, "Lama Zopa Rinpoche's pledge was to work for the happiness of all living beings, and he would break that pledge were he to continue not eating and subsequently die."

Since that fasting period, some thirty years ago, I have never once heard Lama Zopa say that he is hungry or would like to eat. And while his meals are always planned and given to him by his attendants, Lama Zopa Rinpoche often postpones the meal for hours, never really driven by the need to eat. If his attendants did not organize and remind him of his meal, it seems that he might forget or neglect to eat altogether. He is a man with seemingly no worldly desires, including the need to eat and sleep. He is a man who never complains and seems completely content.

Lama Zopa exemplifies another truth about mind training. When we subdue the disturbing emotions of anger, attachment, and desire, we actually become more content than if we were to satisfy all of our wants. For me and many others, Rinpoche exemplifies utter and total selflessness. He is also, like the Dalai Lama, someone who seems to be truly happy every moment of the day. When I say "happy," I do not mean in the sense of being giddy, keyed up, or frivolous. He is totally content and satisfied in each moment.

Lama Zopa recently had a stroke that severely impaired his speech and mobility. However, I never noticed any change in his mood. His attitude was as buoyant as ever, even making fun of himself when he would attempt ordinary actions with his impaired right arm, right leg, or his slurred speech. Sometimes he would attempt to explain something, but his speech would be garbled, and Lama Zopa would just crack up at what would be produced from his mouth.

This is the power of mind training, to face even the reality of illness and death with equanimity and peace.

EXERCISE: THE SPACE MIND

In this exercise, we simply watch our mind work. To begin, do the foundational "You Can Count on It" breath exercise in chapter 1. Once the mind is firmly settled on the breath, imagine your mind as an empty, crystal-clear sky. Then see any thoughts, emotions, sensations, ideas, and voices that arise as appearing like clouds in the sky — some light and wispy, some like thunderheads, maybe an occasional fog bank that rolls through. If no thoughts arise, simply focus on the clear sky as long as possible; this is the mind itself. Do not control the process. Do not hang on to any single cloud-thought, or try to push them away. Don't do anything. Just watch as if you were a child lying on your back in a meadow, looking up at the sky.

THE STOPLIGHT EXERCISE

This is a Space-Mind awareness exercise you can do in your car. Today, while commuting to work or running errands, develop a heightened state of awareness each time you come to a red light or stop sign. Whenever you have to stop, use that as a trigger to check out the "objects" drifting through your mind. With self-awareness, watch where your attention drifts — to another motorist, the people crossing the street, a storefront, maybe a daydream. Then identify and label any emotions that are attached to what you are seeing — attraction, aversion, envy, confusion, and so on. In this exercise, don't do anything with these observations. For now, simply practice identifying the disturbing emotions and mental projections that arise from noticing the imprints of your senses.

CHAPTER FOUR

I'm Mad as Hell,
and I'm Not Going to Take This Anymore

"Everything has mind in the lead,
has mind in the forefront, is made by mind.
If one speaks or acts with a corrupt mind,
misery will follow, as the wheel of a cart follows
the foot of an ox."

— BUDDHA

In this chapter, we look more closely at the Buddha's Second Noble Truth, the causes of suffering. As I've said, the "problem" we seek to solve through mind training is the suffering caused by our own attachment, aversion, and ignorance of the true nature of mind. We may not be able to escape the troubles of the world, but we can exert control over our reactions. Ideally, we can learn to respond in a positive way to any circumstance, and thereby experience peace and contentment no matter what happens.

Any experience triggers a reaction. Mind training helps us determine instantly: Is it a helpful reaction? Then, if it's unhelpful, mind training teaches us how to let go of and even transform this emotion before we act upon it. Our minds are very tricky, however.

Learning to discern unhelpful or negative reactions takes lots of practice and skill. Our reactions may be subtle or coarse, simple or intricate, but if they include what Buddhism calls the "disturbing emotions" — like anger and rage, desire and yearning, ignorance and confusion, and all of their variants — they qualify as "afflictive states" that need to be subdued. Subduing these afflictions means that we take back our life from the negative states of mind that cause suffering. This is like taking back our home after it has been overrun by unwanted guests.

It reminds me of a story my wife tells: When she was about eighteen years old, there was a horrible typhoon in the city of Darwin in the northwest corner of Australia. She lived many hundreds of miles away in Sydney, but the city still received a large stream of refugees seeking shelter there. My wife, being a dutiful citizen and an idealistic young person, allowed a few hippies to camp out on her floor. She didn't charge them rent, and soon the few hippies grew into several, and then several into almost a dozen. Since she had just a three-bedroom apartment, things began to get out of hand. She finally asked them to leave, but they refused. Eventually, she had to move out of the apartment herself.

And so it is with the disturbing emotions. We invite them in because, in the moment, it seems like the right thing to do. Soon, however, they take over our minds and, in truth, don't do a great job at creating a harmonious inner household. So long as there aren't too many, we might be able to tolerate their presence. We work around them; after all, we invited them in the first place. Eventually, inevitably, the disturbing emotions multiply or expand and become unbearable, and if we fail to be assertive, they take over our house.

We have to be wise. We have to spot unwelcome houseguests before they cross our threshold; we have to learn the best strategies for averting disturbing emotions and then for getting rid of them once they arise in our mind. We begin this process by becoming honest judges of our own capacity: How adept are we at handling difficult situations? For us, which situations trigger which disturbing emotions? That is, to use the difficult houseguest analogy: Not all guests cause us the same level of grief, but also, just because we may be able to handle two guests does not mean we can handle twelve. In fact, we may not be able to handle even one truly pain-in-the-ass guest. As this chapter discusses the disturbing emotions, you may recognize that you are much better at handling some than others, and that, for you, certain situations trigger particularly difficult ones. Until you're more practiced with mind training, don't expect to send your worst houseguests packing right away. Know and respect your own boundaries and manage them; managing one's emotional boundaries is a necessary, if temporary, technique. Tackle one emotion at a time, building your skills and strength, knowing that the ultimate goal is to create a mindset that maintains a harmonious outlook no matter how many or how troublesome your houseguests might be, one that stays in balance no matter what is happening "out there."

This obtainable ability to become acutely aware of our inner workings is liberating, yet it requires persistence. Remember: Treasure those "aha!" moments, those flashes of insight into our inner potential, but keep consistently practicing mind training in order to maintain clarity and awareness. I am fond of a quote by the great golfer Ben Hogan: "The more I practice, the luckier I get!" As we know, it is not "luck" at all but the fruitful results of diligent practice. The path of awakening to our inner potential is to become more adroit at applying the awakening tools and reinforcing our natural endowment or ability to let go of our mental afflictions. As the Buddha promised, in this way we end our suffering.

THE THREE DESTRUCTIVE EMOTIONS

In Buddhist psychology, all disturbing emotions arise from just three primary categories: attachment, aversion, and ignorance. Out of these categories arise everything that might trouble us, even if some of these negative states of mind are not, as Westerners might regard them, "emotions" per se. For instance, "ignorance" and "confusion" are listed as disturbing emotions, even though we wouldn't necessarily think of them as "feelings." However, in Buddhist psychology, these negative thoughts or afflictive mental states amount to the same thing as emotions like anger, pride, and fear. They all disturb our equilibrium, and so they are all typically included within the categories of "disturbing," "destructive," or "afflictive" emotions. All these negative thoughts, feelings, and mind states, or "mental stuff," are the focus of mind training, and I've followed this usage and these terms in this book.

In addition, Buddhists are very fond of lists, and you will find numerous variations on these categories of afflictive emotions. This propensity for list-making could be a legacy of the oral history traditions of ancient scholars. In any case, while I prefer to group the disturbing emotions into three primary categories, this isn't the only way to divide them, and the variety of emotions and mental states that they include is almost endless. In fact, some traditional Buddhist texts list as many as eighty-four thousand afflictive emotions and attitudes! Personally, I feel that naming eighty-four thousand afflictive emotions just makes the point that there are seemingly countless variations of the disturbed mind, and the exact number may be equal to the number of living beings on the earth. After all, each person's experience, though similar to others', is still unique.

Thus, in the end, don't get too hung up on categories and terms. It doesn't really matter how these states are categorized. What matters is recognizing them for what they are — as afflictive or disturbing — and then doing our best to be rid of them.

Attachment

The category of "attachment" includes all the emotions that pertain to what we hope for or want to achieve in the world, such as *longing, desire, greediness, ambition, a controlling attitude, a need for power, arrogance, excitation,* and *harmful addictive habits* (like smoking and overeating). Attachment will almost always be signaled by a sense of craving. Also, feelings of *isolation* and *loneliness* would fit under attachment, since we are lonely when we crave to be with others, or with someone we love. Also, afflictions that are considered combinations of attachment and ignorance include *pretension, deception, shamelessness, inconsiderateness of others,* and *distraction.* In fact, there are almost two dozen "secondary afflictions" that are considered extensions of the three "root afflictions" of attachment, aversion, and ignorance.

A very common difficulty in mind training is letting go of desire, and many people wonder: Isn't it a good thing to want a better life and a better world? Isn't love a desire, and if so, does that make love an "affliction"? And further, isn't the desire to improve oneself at the heart of mind training? Indeed, Buddhist psychology makes an important distinction between desire and attachment. One could say that the distinction comes down to *intention.* When desire is directed to a wholesome intention, such as bettering oneself and bettering the world and those around us, then desire can be considered a "useful" affliction. Hope, faith, love, compassion, and empathy are all positive states of mind that Buddhism encourages us to realize. Living them in every moment is the ultimate goal of mind training. These "healthy desires" become "afflictive emotions" when we become attached to outcome, and this is the reason I prefer to call this category "attachment" (rather than "desire," as some have it). In other words, to put this in simple terms, we seek to love others, but with no expectation that they will love us in return. We seek to embody empathy and compassion while letting go and being "unattached" to whether this changes the world around us. We act with the faith that it does and will, but we release any attachment we have to specific outcomes. This can be a very difficult concept to understand and accept, and it will be the focus of the book's final chapter.

Aversion

The emotions that fall under the category of "aversion" are, in one sense, the mirror opposite of the category of attachment, though all these afflictive emotions include an "attachment" to a particular outcome. Typically, aversions are easier to recognize as "negative" states. Instead of wanting or desiring to possess some object, goal, or inner experience, we want to avoid, stop, move away from, or distance ourselves from an object or experience. The emotions that fall under this category include *anger, frustration, rage, meanness, cruelty, irritation, dislike, repulsion, fear, anxiety, resentment, envy or jealousy, impatience, self-hatred, self-loathing,* and *annoyance. Anxiety* or *worry* may not always be the result of an aversion, but they represent a type of fear. For instance, we may be anxious that a party we've planned will go well. In this case, our worry may seem to be "caused" by our attachment to wanting a successful party, but the actual worry arises from an aversion to a negative outcome and the feelings that will generate. Thus, we seek to avoid or move away from that possibility.

Aversion arises when something occurs in the world that we want to deny or avoid or that we disagree with. Aversion is closely connected to discomfort. In fact, we can say it arises in dependence upon discomfort just like attachment arises in dependence upon "comfort" or pleasantness. We may feel discomfort with contrary beliefs, points of view, or ideas. We may feel discomfort with what we consider an unattractive or crass person or with a person from a culture, ethnicity, or background that's strange or unfamiliar to us. Where this gets tricky is that our sense of moral righteousness typically rests on what we judge as "wrong," those things in the world or ourselves that we want to change. In some situations, we might consider our anger as legitimate (and thus "positive"), such as when we feel anger upon encountering a clear injustice like murder or war. However, all anger is considered an afflictive emotion in that it disturbs the mind and needs transforming, no matter how "justified" it is. Indeed, *blame* or *judgment* is another disturbing emotion that falls under the category of aversion (which I will address in more detail below).

A few years ago I was at a conference entitled, interestingly enough, the Happiness Conference. At the conference, two separate speakers described tragically losing a child to violence and how they coped. There was not a dry eye in the venue when the speakers told the horrific details of their stories. In both cases, the perpetrators were arrested, tried, and found guilty. And in both cases, when it came to the penalty phase of the trials, the speakers urged the jury to show compassion and not to impose the death penalty. Both said, at the time, they were urged by others to seek the severest penalty possible, since they were *justified* in their anger and hatred toward the defendants. However, both families had come to realize that anger solved nothing. Anger, bitterness, and revenge were only destroying the families from the inside. Anger and hatred did not harm the defendants, if revenge is what the families sought. And, the families realized, even if they could harm the defendants, where was the benefit? Anger, revenge, and spite had no positive effect on anyone. Admittedly, the pain and suffering the families experienced did not just disappear, but both families stated unequivocally that they believed that, by standing up to their negative emotions, they fared remarkably better, with fewer long-term traumatic effects, than if they had chosen to indulge anger and hate. As a side note, but significantly, because of these demonstrations of compassion, in both

rderers admitted full accountability for their actions
orgiveness from the families.

Ignorance

The topic of ignorance is very complex and profound in Buddhist
thought. Simply put, ignorance of the true nature of reality is the
root of all afflictions. "Reality" means both "How do I exist?" and
"How does the outer world at large exist?" At the same time, this is
somewhat distinct from what's understood by "ignorance" as one of
the three root afflictions, which typically describe more "everyday"
issues like *confusion*, *doubt*, *fogginess*, and *uncertainty*. *Illogical thinking* is a form of ignorance (such as confusing or not understanding
cause and effect), and this can extend to delusional thinking as well
(such as someone who thinks he is a messiah or Jesus). *Blind faith* is
a kind of ignorance. Thinking that what we do has no consequences
is a form of ignorance, as is believing that there are no levels of
reality besides what we can see or touch. Even *forgetfulness* and an
absence of introspection can be forms of ignorance. Ultimately, the
affliction of ignorance is not seeing things clearly, which can include
intuitive insight and logic.

SELF-AWARENESS:
THE MOST EFFECTIVE THERAPY OF ALL

In my therapy practice, I consider any client who walks in the door
seeking counseling for a struggle they are facing to be, in fact, dealing with a disturbing emotion. The person may present their problem as being located in their environment — a bad school system,
the recession, being the victim of a crime, having an abusive childhood, or being addicted to drugs and alcohol. Or they may want
help fixing a relationship or dealing with a difficult or hurtful person
— a cheating partner, an abusive boss, a resentful teenager. And

yet, while I accept that these conditions are challenging and provoking and need attention, my focus is almost entirely on the person's mental state. My goal is to penetrate through the circumstances and identify the disturbing emotions that are driving the client's story. My job is to help my client isolate the disturbing emotions that are manipulating the drama behind the curtain.

To give you an example, here's a sample week from my appointment calendar, which included the following clients:

- Harvey, a partner in a building company, is a coaching client who wanted to discuss getting out of the family business. He was stressed and angry at having to carry most of the burden of a troubled company. He was having problems sleeping at night. His real problem, though, was not the family business, but the disturbing emotions of *fear*, *anxiety*, and *attachment* to success. In Harvey's case, I started with helping him make the transition from locating his problems outside of himself — his unruly family business partners — to seeing that all problems need to be addressed from an internal stance as well. This may sound small, but it is surprising how the majority of clients just do not know how to approach their inner world. In Harvey's case, working with this transition took many sessions. The habit of blaming his partners was very severely entrenched. I believe it was the cause of many of his health issues. As time progressed and he became more attentive to his inner world and more tolerant of his own mental functioning, he was able to generate greater clarity and poise in dealing with his business issues.
- Janet, another business client, is a director of a nonprofit educational program. She was being criticized for her abrasive management style. When we met, she cried, frustrated that no one knew how much she was suffering at not being

accepted and understood by others. Her issue, though, wasn't the lack of empathy from her staff, but her own disturbing emotions of *anger* and *resentment* and *loneliness*. Janet was a fairly self-aware person and, in fact, part of her struggle was knowing she was accountable for her disturbed mind. She knew she could not really blame others for her dis-ease. In Janet's case, it was merely a process of supporting her in further enhancing her own capabilities, of helping her do better at what she already knew how to do. But it can be very helpful to have another set of eyes to help us through the morass created by our confused states of mind.

• Debra, a longtime therapy client, had raised two boys on her own. She often came in for support, to talk to someone so she could feel less isolated and alone. She desperately wanted a companion in her life, but she worried that, at the age of fifty, no man would be interested in her. The disturbing emotions of *worry* or *anxiety*, as well as *self-doubt*, frequently took control of her. These emotions clearly arose from her attachment to having a companion and the wrong belief that another person can make us truly happy. With Debra, the more she examined, and reexamined, her inaccurate belief system, the more she was able to slowly shift her thinking. But this effort also demanded that she pay regular attention to her internal dynamics so that she could head off immediately her habitual longing for a man to free her from loneliness and worry. The more she confronted her attachment, the more the other afflictions subsided.

• In his early forties, Sean still had not really found a career or a long-lasting relationship. He was a loner, but he liked people. He wondered why he could not just commit to one woman and one career choice. On the one hand he feared being tied down, and on the other hand he was not fulfilled.

The disturbing emotion of *attachment*, particularly his concept of what kind of lifestyle would make him happy (and thus who he needed to be in that lifestyle), was strangling him and preventing him from stepping into a greater sense of his potential. First, I helped him see that his belief in his dream lifestyle was really a type of ignorance. And like all the disturbing emotions, it was a negative habit that resided within his mind and that actually undermined his happiness, causing him problems. Then, I helped him develop his awareness of his habitual beliefs and thinking, so he could stand up to and not engage in the usual pattern. Then he could exercise a more "preferred self," one he chose to be.

- Julie had continuing health problems, many of which remained undiagnosed. As a result of her difficulties, her thinking would become muddled and she was unable to make decisions. As she said, "This drives me crazy because in the past I was very decisive." Illness and its effects upon our mental state are one of the most difficult precipitators. While there is a powerful interconnection between body and mind, our focus in mind training is attending to our mental well-being. Even if illness or the body is causing us turmoil, we still have to confront and deal with the internal effects from an internal approach. Often, just attending to the physical aspect of the problem does not offer lasting relief. Thus, in Julie's case, *ignorance* and *confusion* were the primary disturbing emotions arising for her. The effects of her illness, plus the insecurity and confusion that arose from a lack of diagnosis, sapped her mental strength and capabilities. In Julie's case, the best intervention was helping her to generate a state of clarity through a continual application of mindfulness practices like those presented in the early chapters of this book.

Per the examples above, once the client and I have labeled a primary or dominating afflictive emotion, the next step is to invite the client to learn and study the emotion as it arises in the various arenas of their life. It is essential that the client becomes familiar with the intricacies, strategies, and trickeries of the afflictive emotion. Remember, only the client can really heal him- or herself, and thus the client is, ultimately, the therapist. I hold the conviction that to *really* understand psychology we have to understand *our* psychology. To study psychology is to study ourselves. And by studying ourselves we increase our wisdom-understanding — the most effective therapeutic intervention of them all!

PRACTICE HONESTY WITHOUT GUILT

When I was first introduced to these ideas and began investigating my own mind through introspection, I felt that the disturbing emotion of anger was not really all that present in my own mindstream. I had always prided myself on being someone who was not an angry person, and I suppose on a relative level that was somewhat true. I had other afflictions that I knew I struggled with, but anger did not really present itself as a problem for me.

However, as I became more and more familiar with the workings of my mind and emotions, I realized that — while I wasn't someone who flew into wild rages — I nonetheless had a whole ocean of anger below the surface. This would typically present itself as irritation, impatience, frustration, and annoyance. Then, as I delved even deeper in my investigation of my inner nature, I found that, if I wasn't thinking of something I wanted, then I was thinking of something I didn't want. Far more than I realized, I found my mind focused on unpleasant consequences I wanted to avoid, and this gave rise to all sorts of disturbing emotions that are related to the branch of afflictive emotion we call "anger." To my disappointment, I found that I was really quite frequently irritated or uneasy, even though I was not conscious of the fact. Even today, I can still sometimes look back at a typical morning and realize with some shock that all I've done is slip from one annoyed, irritated, frustrated thought to the next: a barking dog wakes me too early, my coffee is cold, the waitress is surly, a phone call interrupts my concentration, and so on.

I've been doing this a long time, and it would be very easy for me to get down on myself: Why aren't I better at this? But this kind of reaction is a trap. If we did this, we'd simply be doubling down on our frustration by also shaming ourselves. We'd only be increasing our disturbing emotions. We need to be honest when examining ourselves, but we can't then use what we find to make ourselves feel worse through guilt, shame, disappointment, embarrassment, or despair.

We are trying to develop a different relationship with our mind. Awareness contributes to the subduing of the harmful emotions, and this awareness extends to everything, including ourselves. We need to treat ourselves with the same objective distance that a therapist uses for her clients. By subduing the harmful emotions and afflictive states of mind, our aim is to increase our helpful emotions or mental states, like empathy, gentleness, compassion, wisdom, generosity, warmth, and so on. The more we become aware of our inner workings, the more adept we become at applying the mental balancing techniques that will offer us true mental health. The truth is, though, that it can sometimes be easier to apply them as they relate to others than to ourselves. However, if we can engage the disturbing emotions in a curious, open-hearted manner, without guilt or judgment, then we can more easily subdue them and, in turn, experience the positive emotions and attitudes that accompany a balanced and healthy mind. A healthy mind *is* generous, warm, caring, and wise. If we find we are not extending those qualities to ourselves, then we are still under the tyranny of our afflictions. As we develop our mindfulness, we become increasingly aware, both in frequency and depth, of the arisings of the various mental states throughout the day.

BLAME VERSUS ACCOUNTABILITY

Blame looms large in our litigious society. The entire insurance industry is built on the assignment of blame. America is famously a country of "laws," and the American legal system is dedicated to distinguishing right and wrong, cause and effect. We could even say each of us has an internalized judge and jury eager to dispense "justice" in every situation.

Thus, many Westerners can have a hard time with the techniques of mind training that seem to let people "off the hook." Surely, we think: If someone hits me, and I feel pain and anger, I am not responsible for my feelings. They did something to me, so how can I be "wrong" to be angry? And if I let go of my anger, then what happens to the person who hit me? Where's the justice in that? Are we supposed to just accept any abuse we receive? As we saw above, we include ourselves in this cycle of judgment as well: If I fail at something, then aren't I correct to be disappointed and angry at myself?

This is a complex issue, and yet resolving it is essential to our ultimate success. Simply put, the solution is to understand the crucial difference between blame and accountability:

- *Blame* is a destructive emotion that expresses our anger, hostility, and desire to move the problem off ourselves and onto anywhere else, even upon someone else. Blame is a form of punishment. No real, positive learning can come from blame, which almost inevitably is either hurtful or polarizing.
- *Accountability* is an objective acknowledgment of our (or another's) actions. It is a nonemotional assessment of one's

role in an event, and it is the way we take responsibility for our actions.

At times, the distinction between blame and accountability can seem like splitting hairs, and it's almost useless turning to our society for guidance. Do you remember the McDonald's "hot coffee" lawsuit several years ago? A woman bought a cup of coffee at McDonald's, and minutes later, as she was driving, she spilled the coffee on herself and received severe burns on her legs. She filed a lawsuit and was eventually awarded about $600,000 in damages. So who was to blame? The McDonald's franchise for making the coffee scalding hot? Corporate headquarters for printing the warning label too small to read easily? The woman for holding the coffee in her lap while driving? The person in the McDonald's restaurant who actually filled the cup and gave it to her and might have warned her to be careful? As we can see, many factors contributed to the woman's injury; there was accountability on many sides. But any sense of a fair accounting usually gets lost in our legal system, which is solely focused on assigning blame between two competing parties and meting out the appropriate punishment.

When we consider the blame dynamic as it works in our interior or emotional life, we see that blame's strategies become more subtle, and perhaps more dangerous. One of blame's harmful tricks is to turn the blame inward. This inward blame doesn't just identify a mistake or error, but goes out of its way to make ourselves feel defective. Blame can also become our "excuse" for giving up or not trying:

- "I am still so overweight. I hate myself for looking this way. I'll never be able to diet."
- "What's wrong with me that I can't remember the five things I need to buy at the supermarket? I'm so stupid."

- "I'm so anxious about this dinner party tonight. I never tell funny stories. I'm just not much fun to be with, I guess, which must be why I have so few friends."
- Working mothers might think, "I'd probably get along with my resentful teenage son if only I hadn't gone back to work so soon after he was born."

The other "trick" blame pulls is that we use it to escape true personal accountability: instead of acknowledging our part in our own suffering, we blame others or the world. We blame our parents for the way they raised us; we blame our lover for being unfaithful or for not loving us enough or in the way we want; we blame the government or God or natural disasters for our problems and unhappiness. We say, "I could be successful and happy, if only X hadn't happened" or "if only X *would* happen!" Sometimes, indeed, our problems can feel so overwhelming that it just seems too painful to think that, on some level, we are responsible for our feelings, our experience. Shifting the blame then becomes a way to soothe our hurts by spreading our misery.

Thus, in all these ways, blame is a trap that undermines our success and happiness. One of the results of giving in to blame is that we treat ourselves like victims. It is a way of saying that bad things have happened to us, either by forces "out there" or by our own hands, and we cannot help being unhappy because of it. We "justify" our suffering, and we cling to those justifications, even though they prevent us from feeling better. This is why it can be so hard to let our suffering go. We have to give up self-righteousness.

For instance, I once hired an amateur tree cutter who accidentally dropped a eucalyptus tree on my roof. I was livid and wanted him to do hard time in San Quentin. *But anger is internal, and thus the cause of my suffering was internal.* The poor guy cost me thousands of dollars in roof repair, and this was a circumstance I had to deal with. He was certainly responsible for his mistake and the damage it caused, but he was not responsible for my anger. Any disturbing emotion always arises internally, and so we are always accountable for our emotional reactions, our internal stuff, and for any actions that are generated by our emotions. I could have clapped him on the back reassuringly and told him we'd figure out a solution (after all, I'd just learned a valuable, if expensive, lesson about hiring amateur tree cutters), or I could have yelled at him for an hour, red in the face, and then brought a lawsuit. Which action would have increased both of our suffering, and which would have diminished it?

When we catch ourselves "blaming," our job is to recognize this as a disturbing emotion and become aware of where the blame is originating from. The material world is an endless source of difficult circumstances and challenges. These are only external conditions, however. They only become "problems" when we label them as such, just like the umpires. The only true "problems" we have are the disturbing emotions, which obscure the true nature of mind and cause us to act out of confusion and ignorance, increasing our own suffering and that of others.

As the example above makes clear, if we can see our disturbing emotions as the true cause of our suffering, and attack those so that we overcome them, then *we gain control of our mind*, and our actions become more effective. Let's take another example: say you're attending your favorite niece's wedding, and during the reception, her mother (your sister) comes up to you and says, "We scheduled a time for you to offer a little talk right after we make the toast." If you, like roughly 85 percent of the population, are terrified of public speaking, then your reaction may be one of fear and anxiety. You love your niece, but you don't want to make a fool of yourself. You start downing champagne to calm your nerves, but your palms are sweating, your stomach is in a knot, and your thoughts are racing. You suddenly can't think of a single interesting thing to say about your niece, but there are all sorts of things you'd like to say about your sister, none of them good. Out of habit, you displace your discomfort by blaming her: "How could my sister ask me to do this at the last minute? She knows I hate public speaking. She's so inconsiderate and always thinking only of herself. She's bossing me around just like when we were kids, always dominating me and telling me what to do." Even if you are partly right, you are now wasting what little time you have to prepare a nice speech by giving in to your blame and anger at your sister. And then what would happen if you discovered later that your niece had been too shy to ask you herself, so she had asked her mom to do it? And so on it goes throughout our life.

We have a tendency to place blame in such a way that it hinders us from being effective and resolving recurring conflicts. When we identify or "fuse" with a disturbing emotion or mental state, we almost become blind. We lose our ability to influence a situation, and frequently we act in ways that perpetuate or worsen troubles. In a way, our sense of self and the emotion appear to us as one; we think our anger *is* us. But a finger cannot scratch an itch on itself; we are in a mental straitjacket. Irritation or frustration is one of the easiest disturbing emotions in which to see this dynamic at work. When we are frustrated, unable to get what we want or are getting exactly what we don't want, we become increasingly powerless the more frustrated we become. We will explore this dynamic and our sense of self more closely in chapter 7.

BLAME AND EFFECTIVENESS

Since the line between blame and accountability can at times appear narrow — that is, until we become more discerning — we can learn to recognize them by the results of our actions. As I indicate above, one of the most important aspects of this dynamic is that, almost without fail, blame leads to ineffective action, while accountability

leads to effective action. This is reassuring. It means mind training doesn't just help us "feel better"; it's a practical, pragmatic approach to problem-solving.

Perhaps the most dangerous theory, prevalent since the first
days of modern psychology, is the concept that our current mental conflicts are a result of the way our parents treated us or, more
broadly, the way we were brought up, our childhood. To a degree,
this idea of blaming our parents for our psychological problems has
become less prevalent, but it remains popular in our general culture — maybe even more popular today than when Freud and his
old cronies first promoted the idea. So often it seems that when
a child acts out or gets into trouble, people automatically think,
"What kind of parents does he have? His mother must not be giving him the attention he needs. His father must be disengaged and
critical." Therapists are still trained to examine the parenting dynamics of patients to find the causes of a disorder. The manner of
blaming our parents takes on different forms, but these are merely
a different set of clothes on the same old villain. We develop bad
emotional habits we are unable to quit, and we point to our alco-
holic family, dysfunctional family, absent father, single mother,
nonbreastfeeding mother, blended family, divorced family, abusive
father and mother, and on and on as the reason. Where does this
finger-pointing get us?

I do not dismiss the seriousness of these situations, nor am I
trying to minimize their impact. I have worked with many, many
abused children and domestic partners; they are not to be blamed
for the abuse they have suffered at the hands of their caregivers and
partners. But as adults, we are each responsible for our own interior
lives. We are accountable for our mental health and emotions, even
if we are not to "blame" or accountable for our circumstances growing up. But if we don't accept that accountability for ourselves, then
we only perpetuate the abuse of the past. We are the only ones who

can heal our mind, and all of us have healing to do. Understanding our past can be helpful, but even that is not necessary. To eliminate the causes of our suffering, we need to attend to each moment differently than we have in the past. We need to control and deal with the disturbing emotions arising in the moment. The past contributed, yes, but if we want to eliminate the causes of our disturbing emotions, our hurt, our anxiety, our sense of fear, and lack of safety, we need to turn our attention inward. Until we do, we will never fully alleviate our pain. Never.

Similarly, people often point out, and rightly, that the world is full of real, serious, ongoing problems that affect the well-being of everyone. I do not deny this. Exploitation of less-empowered workers, misuse of our environmental resources, using violence to solve conflict, and marginalization of less-privileged people are just a few examples of the difficult conditions we face. Each of us should indeed work to make the world a better place, on behalf of and along with our fellow global brothers and sisters. However, we don't solve these problems by "blaming" them for our own unhappiness and unhealthy emotions. We can, and should, turn this around and say: There would be no abusive parenting if parents were not taken over by anger, rage, frustration, ignorance, and self-centeredness. There would be no violence if everyone embodied an attitude of tolerance and serenity. Workers would not be marginalized and taken advantage of if each of us focused on compassionate generosity, rather than self-centered greed. The funny and encouraging thing is, the more we tame the aggression and conflict within our own being, the more we are able to attend to the needs of our community. Inner peace truly is the path to world peace. This doesn't mean we stop working to make things better and change the harmful conditions in the world, but we need to do so from a mindset and inner motivation of empathy, compassion, and peace. As Mahatma Gandhi so aptly said, "An eye for an eye leaves the whole world blind." Responding to anger with anger does not bring peace or healing. Thus, training our mind and healing ourselves are, I would argue, the only way to bring lasting change to the world around us. We can only do this when we drop blame and simply become accountable for subduing and training our mind and mental attitudes.

By using the four steps of mind training that I present, we familiarize ourselves with the misleading mind and its cohorts, the disturbing emotions, and we begin to approach the disturbing emotions differently. We develop more poise and become less reactive as they arise. We are able to pause before we impulsively respond to their usual demands. At times, the disturbing emotions can be seen as symptoms, like sneezing when we have a cold, and we just let them arise and fall away without their usual charge. As we develop our minds and engage in mental fitness, we begin to relate to everything that arises inwardly in a more curious manner. We begin, more and more, to relate to ourselves as learners, and all that arises becomes lessons in developing our mind.

EXERCISE: BECOME ACQUAINTED

In order to act more mindfully, we have to become more acquainted with ourselves. For this exercise, in successive weeks, you will pay close attention to how often you experience disturbing emotions and then how often you experience positive emotions.

For the first week, each hour you will pause for a moment and just notice, and notate, any pain, irritation, or discomfort you have felt over the past hour, both emotional and physical. Carry around a notebook and jot down your notations; these are meant to be quick, but try to record the context, duration, and strength of the emotions or mind states. It is best to do this for at least five days so that you can begin to get a sense of what your "norm" is like. Then, when you go to bed at night, take note before you turn out the light.

The following week, focus on your experience of happiness or satisfaction. Every hour, perhaps using a reminder alarm on your mobile phone or PDA, take a minute to jot down and reflect on when you have felt good and in control over the past hour.

At the end of the two weeks, spend some time reviewing each week's notations and breaking down what you have recorded into a series of lists. There is no set format you need to follow. The goal is to simply become more familiar with yourself, so tally and categorize what you find in whatever way gives you the best perspective on your actual in-the-moment experience each day.

As you evaluate your separate logs, ask yourself the same series of questions for both positive and negative states of mind:

How often do they occur?
How long do they last?
Are there any obvious triggers?
Are there any obvious patterns?
How much control do you have?

This exercise is merely to increase awareness. Ideally, however, this list will reveal your emotional "habits." With this, you no longer need to wait for problems to arise to practice mind training. You can anticipate those situations that trigger certain emotions and be ready to practice mind training so you can change those habits you don't like, as well as strengthen the good ones.

CHAPTER FIVE

What in the World Is Going On?

In the last two chapters, we've discussed how our emotions, and in fact all thoughts, concepts, and experiences, arise within our mind. Mainly, we have been focused on locating the correct source of our "problem," which is, in essence, the mental stuff that exists in our own mind. Circumstances and events occur, and we react to them, and if we don't recognize when disturbing emotions are guiding our reactions, we experience unhappiness and suffering.

Buddhism maintains that, in fact, *all* disturbing emotions and problems arise from our misperception of how things really exist. When we are unable to understand the way things really are, that's when a myriad of difficulties arise. As a Buddhist teacher of mine, Geshe Gelek, has said, "We see things that are not there, and do not see things that are there."

So what is it that we *really* experience when we see things and interact with the world around us? What is the divide between what exists "out there" and what is "in our heads"? The next several chapters look at this more closely. For if we can understand the mechanics of how we construct our reality, then we will be better able to *apply appropriate countermeasures to eliminate disturbing emotions when they arise.* For it is the correct perception of things as they are, of reality, that will free us from constantly being whipsawed by whatever emotion may arise within our mind. Thus, in Buddhism, "ignorance" simply equals "not seeing things as they really are," and "wisdom" equals "seeing things as they are," which is the ultimate remedy to all our problems. How liberating to think of having a mind that can do whatever we wish it to do!

This is not some kind of fantasy. It is possible to slowly improve the quality of our mind, just as others have done before us. To do so, we have to be open, curious, courageous, and willing to become learners again. These attributes of courage and curiosity allow us to view troublesome mind states as simply learning material for transforming our lives into deeper and more meaningful pursuits.

In actuality, things and events, feelings and thoughts, are not nearly as concrete and "existent" as they seem. That is really the whole point of trying to discern what reality is and then living our lives with this new perception of the world and ourselves within it. If we understand things and events, feelings and thoughts, to be merely constructed and dependent upon our own mental concepts, then they will exert much less power over us. For we will come to realize that not only are we the *constructors* of our reality, but we can also be the *transformers* of our reality.

THE SCAFFOLDING OF OUR
CONSTRUCTED REALITIES

When we examine the scaffolding of our constructed realities, problems lose their hold and start to seem a lot more like clouds and mist and less like concrete and steel. We construct our reality in a variety of ways. From past experiences, we form opinions and conclusions — about ourselves, the world, and the past and future. This is how we create meaning and build knowledge, using every experience we have. But this process can also lead us to make some false assumptions, and when this happens, we construct meaning based upon a misconstruing of reality. We see things as permanent, when they are changing; we see things as unified, when they are an infinite collection of parts; we see things and ourselves as independent, autonomous entities, when all is interdependent and related. And most of all, we superimpose the sum total of our past experiences and beliefs onto the present moment and keep ourselves from seeing the truth of what's right before our eyes.

From the perspective of Buddhist psychology, our standard perception of reality is warped. It may seem like we are born with minds that are pure and clear, and in fact the child's mind is less concrete and fixed. But nonetheless we have the imprints and seeds lying dormant that will arise to further obscure our view of reality. All of our thoughts are a kind of cloudiness, and as young children, we are initially unable or unaware enough to distinguish them. Our thoughts are just "us," and we assume they accurately reflect reality. This view is then reinforced by life lessons and the world around us. Our conception of self and the world is strongly influenced by our environments, by our cultures, social groups, families, friends, and so on. The social and cultural values, and the incessant messages we receive, condition us to regard reality in certain incorrect ways. We are constantly bombarded with messages of the way things are. We are encouraged to believe that what has occurred predicts what will occur, and that it is possible to know reality independent of our limited view of it. We are taught, in other words, that we can rely on our individual experience to "know" reality (when all we really know are the concepts and projections in our mind).

For instance, as a child we are taught the difference between "right" and "wrong." We are taught, perhaps, to have realistic expectations about what we can and cannot achieve in life. We learn who others consider "good people" and who are "bad people." In short, we are taught to make sense of things by imposing our judgment on everything in front of us. Naturally, as we grow up, we question some of the judgments and interpretations thrown our way; we agree with some and disagree with others, and fit our personal understandings to our experience. But we rarely question the act of judging itself. Without much analysis, we simply keep interpreting and reinterpreting reality as good or bad, right or wrong, useful or detrimental, fun or boring, constantly tweaking our conceptions as new experiences reinforce or undermine what we think we "know."

What are some of these conceptions? They might pertain to who we think we are: "I hate flying; planes are so uncomfortable." Or, "I'm terrible at math." Or, "I want to get married and have children." Our concepts might have to do with other people or the world: "True love just happens." "My soul mate is out there somewhere." "Cities aren't safe at night." Some of our beliefs have the appearance of direct observation, like saying, "The light has turned green." But if we become frustrated because the car in front of us doesn't move when the light changes, we realize that we have embellished our observation with a host of assumptions, projections, and expectations: "A green light means go forward without hesitating, especially when I'm in a hurry, or else you must be the type of idiot driver I knew would get in my way!" If we expect "idiot drivers" to thwart us at every turn, we are virtually assuring that we will "see" idiot drivers in the present moment, and "like always," they will make us insane. If we can learn to become aware of and then become suspicious of the "truth" of our assumptions and projections, we can start to glimpse how things really are, and we can begin to understand how self-defeating so much of what we "know" actually is. There is such a depth and vastness of variables and conditions that lead up to every moment of experience that if we were to see even an iota of all these factors, we would, simply put, act with far more wisdom, compassion, and effectiveness.

An interesting story illustrates this dynamic:

In January 2007, a scruffy man in jeans, T-shirt, and baseball cap emerged from the subway in Washington, DC, and lifted a violin to his chin. It was the height of the morning rush hour, and 1,097 people passed by during the forty-three minutes that the man played. It took six minutes before anyone stopped to listen, and by the end, the man collected a total of $32.17. One child walked past who was visibly drawn to the music, but who was then dragged away by the adult accompanying him. This was no ordinary street performer, however. This was an experiment organized by the *Washington Post* (later published as "Pearls Before Breakfast" by Gene Weigarten on April 8, 2007) to see whether Joshua Bell — one of the most accomplished musicians in the world, and playing six of the most sensational pieces in the violin repertoire on a priceless Stradivarius — was capable of distracting people from their headlong rush to work.

In other words: Would anyone recognize world-class artistry out of context? This potent story captures the truth that, more often than not, *we see our projections rather than what is really there*. While it's impossible to know what each of the 1,097 people thought as they passed, we can be relatively assured that most shared some similar assumptions, such as: master musicians do not play in the subway hustling for change during rush hour. Indeed, how many of those commuters who tossed in a buck would have gladly paid $100 for the same concert if they'd known who it was? Surely the $32.17 Bell earned in the subway was not a comment on his reputation or skill. It was a reflection of where he performed and the people's assumptions in their "rush hour" heads. The only people who play in subways, we assume, are amateurs who can't get real gigs. And the cost of their concerts? Spare change; perhaps a few bucks if we're really impressed.

Still, if no one recognized Joshua Bell or the priceless instrument he held, wouldn't they, almost despite themselves, respond to the music itself? Despite the environment, wouldn't the masterful quality of the music and the performer's talent be self-evident, inescapable, obvious to anyone? Naturally, this gets into tricky territory. By most criteria, Joshua Bell is one of the world's most talented musicians, but not everyone would agree, nor would everyone value violin music to the same extent. Like our three umpires, we call our own balls and strikes, and so what some label merely "adequate" others label "great." Still, to judge by the majority of the people in the subway station that day, they weren't acting based on their evaluation of the artistic merit of the music they were hearing. No, what seems obvious is that most weren't hearing the music at all, at least not directly or "objectively." They were so "in their heads," so full of their early-morning anticipation for the day, and so confident in their prejudged assessment of "subway buskers" that they weren't even listening. Their minds were trapped in their projected context and only heard the music they expected to hear.

CHARACTERS IN A DRAMA

Another reason we do not see things as they are in the present moment is because we get caught up in our own internal dialogues or dramas. Using our past experience and the feedback of our family, community, and the whole gamut of social influences, we construct personal (and even social) narratives. In these, we embody a multiplicity of characters to fit the multitude of narratives we create. In fact, it is more appropriate to say that these narratives create us, our identities. These narratives use all kinds of props to maintain their "reality," and the people around us — society and media — all contribute information supporting these narratives or descriptions of who we are, who everyone else is, and how the world exists at large. Whatever our "narrative," we and everyone involved are contributors — as with an epic film, the credits are quite extensive.

Everyone tends to become identified with various narratives, be it "victim," "rescuer," "expert," "parent," "lover," "abuser," and so on. Out of this, we tend to see people, events, and emotional states as permanent, fixed, and unchanging. This tendency causes us no end of trouble.

For instance, we frequently identify people in simplistic terms, based on a personal trait or particular experience. We talk of people in static terms: "He is so stubborn," "She is so kind," "That kid is trouble," "She is so needy." Of course, we all have tendencies and idiosyncrasies and certain things that make us unique. But we fall into traps when we label people in concrete terms and come to expect them to act in certain ways, invariably and always. It can be easy to see this in the abstract, and yet it's an extremely common mistake. We come to our mother expecting loving understanding because she has "always" shown us that, and we come to rely on her to provide this for us, and one day she's curt and judgmental. We react in shock and anger, and blame her for being uncaring, but our anger and hurt are our clues that the problem is inside our own mind. We've acted as if our narrative *is* the real world, and we are unable to see and accept our mother as she is.

We do the exact same thing to ourselves. If we grow up in a family where we hear over and over that we're not going to amount to anything, that we're lazy, then that becomes one of our "stories." Our personal self-image gets frozen. These labels become who we think we actually are, and we live in reaction to them. This reactive mode can take many forms: we might respond by trying to either prove our family wrong or prove them right. But whatever happens, we interpret every event through the projections of our personal narrative or inner dialogue: "The reason I can't change jobs is because I'm lazy and worthless," or "If I'm not the best at everything, I'm just being lazy and worthless, like my family always said I was."

In narrative theory, when we pigeonhole others into static roles and treat them like fixed, unchanging entities, it is said we "totalize" them. We do this by ignoring, or being ignorant of, the constant shifting nature of people and all life and thus lose sight of all the exceptions that exist to the "totalizing" description of the other person. We are quite literally physically different each passing day, and in each moment, we are capable of choosing any reaction. Nothing is predetermined or fixed, particularly in our emotional life. As therapists, we are constantly challenging a client's totalizing of him- or herself and others. And, as therapists, we should constantly challenge our own totalizing of ourselves as therapists and our clients as clients.

This process of totalizing is pervasive and defies reality. We may judge and blame someone for hurting us, and yet we know very little of other people, of their motivations and situation. Often, we admit we know very little of what motivates ourself. So why do we judge with such assurance and conviction? Why are we so quick to blame something or someone for our suffering? If a bank teller messes up our transaction, and we think, "She's sure lousy at her job," we have totalized her. It doesn't matter why we did, or how this judgment fits our expectations and projections of life. It's just important, in the moment, to see *that* we did and to undo this projection for our own peace of mind. A great aid in this, though it's not 100 percent necessary, is to understand why she made a mistake: perhaps she's new in her job, or she is a mother preoccupied with worry over a sick daughter. Perhaps she is an otherwise ideal, skilled employee, and we were unlucky to catch her on a "bad day." Knowing a situation more fully is one of the components of generating compassion and empathy. However, whether we understand more fully the context of the situation or not, we have to be aware of our projections and our disturbing emotions in the moment. As we let go of them, and their hold upon us lessens, we heal our suffering in that moment. However, if we don't see our own process of projecting, then no explanation of the teller will solve our real dilemma.

Why is totalizing incorrect? Take fog, for example: It is a constantly moving and shifting mass of gray vapor, but it is not *only*, totally gray. It has other colors. It has moisture. It's made up of countless parts and aspects, all moving and swirling. It would be more accurate to say, and perceive, that fog *has* gray rather than to say fog *is* gray. This is not just semantics. There is a huge difference between perceiving something *as* a characteristic rather than as *having* a characteristic. Even something as simple as fog can be quite complex to grasp in its totality, and this is even more true with people.

Here's another real-life example: The other day I was playing golf. It was a holiday, and the course was crowded and slow. What would typically be a four-hour round was taking five and a half hours. The golf club has marshals on the course to help keep things speedy and efficient, but on this day it wasn't working. Some in our party started to grumble. Someone asked, "Who's marshaling?" Someone else said, "Who do you think? Paul!" Everyone groaned. Everyone always groans when Paul marshals because, well, he's just *too* nice for the job. One person called him "very inept," and another exclaimed, "He doesn't know what the hell he is doing." Another player grumbled, "Yeah, I think he is senile." This was followed by a number of grunts and groans of agreement.

Among the eight of us was one woman, who was playing in my foursome. She was the wife of another player. She took a risk and blurted out, "Oh, Paul! He's my favorite. He's the guy who always has a bag of candy and is never in a grumpy mood!" I was so pleasantly struck by her comment. Her perception was entirely different from the rest, and she reminded us that Paul exists the way he appears to each of us individually. As I found out later, Paul is a senior citizen they hired because he was on the verge of homelessness.

Without his golf-course job, Paul might have to resort to panhandling on the street corner. As we know, the "narrative" of homelessness equals utter failure as a productive member of society. As "one of those guys with a sign asking for help," Paul would become nothing but a totalized projection for passersby, for the "rest of us."

Seeing things as static and then totalizing them are not the same thing, but they are interrelated. We can be fooled and see things as static without totalizing them, but we cannot totalize things without first seeing them as static.

LOVE STORIES

This dynamic of how we layer reality with our projections and assumptions is never more clear than in the realm of romance and relationships. Just about every love story ever written has, at its dramatic center, the belief that we need someone else in our life to be happy. And not just any someone, of course, but that one particular person who alone is "right" for us, our "soul mate." How is this love mistaken? Let me count the ways.

First, of course, only we control our own happiness because all suffering and happiness are products of mind. Thus, if happiness, love, and compassion are states of mind, then we are responsible for them in ourselves. This isn't to dismiss the power of love, which is transformative, but it transforms our own heart before it can transform the hearts of others.

Another mistake is that we forget that the other person struggles from their own afflictions. If we totalize the other as our ideal of beauty and loving kindness, they are bound to disappoint us, for they are imperfect, as we all are. In addition, should the other person accept this role in our drama, and believe their job is to ensure our happiness, they are bound to fail, for not only can't they control what may happen in the future, but they certainly can't control what goes on in our mind. Indeed, anyone who has experienced unrequited love knows that no amount of affection or desire can influence someone else if they've "made up their mind" against us.

Consider the case of Jay, one of my clients. Like so many Americans, Jay believed that falling in love with the perfect mate was the key to happiness. He had had a crush on Wendy since he was a boy, and when he learned that she was divorcing her husband of thirty-five years, he saw an opportunity to finally have what he had always wanted and be happy. Jay and Wendy got married. Although they were financially secure, Wendy asked Jay to sell the house he loved so that they could "buy a house of their own." However, one year later, they went through a bitter divorce. Their love turned to such hatred and pain that Wendy cut off all contact with Jay, and to this day he doesn't know her whereabouts.

Jay acted on the basis of a number of serious — and, unfortunately, quite common — misperceptions. First, he believed he needed one particular person to be happy. He thought of Wendy as his soul mate. But even more, he had "frozen" his image of Wendy from childhood, along with his "vision" of what marriage to her would be like. Both of these projections meant he was blind to their current reality. Jay and Wendy were now very different people (and even when he created his image of her in their youth, this was still a limited projection of Wendy). In fact, they were continuing to change moment to moment. Wendy was no longer the physical "beauty" Jay originally fell in love with, and in this and other ways, she failed to live up to the ideal of her he had cultivated for years. Wendy suffered from her own afflictions, but Jay shielded himself from this "ugly truth."

Or take the case of Amanda, another client. Amanda is, ostensibly, in a stable marriage with a loyal, committed husband, except that she suffers from a wide range of disturbing emotions: jealousy, fear, anxiety, and more. Amanda becomes depressed and despondent when her husband goes out of town on business, for she believes that she cannot handle being alone. That is one of the "narratives" or "stories" that dominate her — that she needs her husband's physical presence to feel safe and comforted. Then, when he is away, she can't contain her fear, which is that he will cheat on her with another woman, even though he has always been faithful. Amanda cannot seem to stop projecting her insecurities onto her husband in a way that torments her night after night until he returns home. Amanda sees things not as they are or as she would like them to be but as she fears they will be.

Amanda has subscribed to the common belief that her husband is the source of her well-being and can provide her with the happiness she needs. Until she is free of this narrative, her suffering is inevitable, for neither her husband nor the security he offers is permanent, unchanging, and static. What happens if her husband dies before her, or if, tired of being mistrusted, he leaves her or cheats on her (thus accepting the role her fears have "cast" him in)? Amanda is setting herself up for a fall. She has put herself in someone else's hands; her mind, never satisfied and relying upon the wrong object, will continue to create dissatisfaction until Amanda changes her mistaken perception — until she realizes that her mistaken perception is the source of her happiness and her pain.

STUCK IN TRAFFIC

One aspect of this distorted perspective, explained extensively in Buddhist psychology, is that we come to regard people, things, events, and even thoughts and feelings as independent realities or entities. Nothing exists independently. First, as we've seen, our perception labels and colors reality, so we can't know anything as it is in any truly objective, independent way. This is true for us, and it's true for everyone. Everyone's perspective is partial, and there is always a larger context to everything that happens — but we forget this. We see the world fragmentally, like the jerky images of a slide show, but we act as if we are directors of a movie, as if we could predict and shape the arising flow of experience.

For instance, ask yourself, how calm are you in traffic? Do you ever suffer from road rage? If you are someone who never gets agitated while driving, my hat's off to you. But most of us find it extremely difficult to maintain our sense of emotional balance on the road, and some people literally go insane at the mere possibility that they will be five minutes late. However, traffic is a perfect arena to practice tolerance of unpredictability, and acceptance of our lack of control, while remaining calm.

According to news reports, road rage is on the rise, but why? Today, there are more vehicles on the road, more people driving, and more congestion than ever before. Armed with this knowledge, why do we still get so uptight, angry, and frustrated when we encounter traffic? Shouldn't we expect it? Or is expecting it part of the problem? Could it be the way we see the situation? If we saw it differently, would it help? In truth, "bad traffic" does not exist as some independent entity like we think it does. It exists only in its relationship to oneself.

Traffic is only "bad" within the larger context of our labels, assumptions, and expectations. When are we the most frustrated by traffic? When we are trying to get somewhere specific at an exact time. We have "plans," sometimes "important" plans; to be late could upset an entire world of desires and needs and expectations, which we share with the people expecting us. Then, when we encounter "bad traffic," our desires get thwarted, the future we've conceived of and planned for is threatened, and we experience rage at this loss of control. The strength of our emotional reaction is typically equivalent to the rigidity of our concepts.

Consider the opposite: What happens on a road trip, when you have no firm destination or timetable? Maybe, as cars back up and everyone slows to a crawl, you get annoyed, but your expectation is to "enjoy the road," so you do. You don't have a fixed timetable. You go with the flow, or take a scenic detour, and let your annoyance go. Thus, our experience of "traffic" is directly related to the mental picture we created, consciously or subconsciously, before we left our house or office. And that mental picture we created before leaving our house is just a further elaboration of earlier mental pictures. We become attached to our concept of the way things "should be," or the way we want them to happen. This concept seems independent and real, and the "bad traffic" that thwarts us seems independent and real, but we do not see that both are part of a drama existing only in our head, the sum of our history, our hopes, and the expectations of the countless other people who are involved.

Thus, there is no such thing as "bad traffic" in any independent sense. If so, then everyone in a traffic jam would experience it that way. But they don't. Of course, there are cars, there is a road, there are traffic lights. In other words, there is some kind of "data." But people experience this data differently and the experience is believed to be "real." Some people might enjoy the extra time to make phone calls, others may not care how fast they go, and some might pass the time listening to their book on tape.

Like the fog we talked about earlier, there is a physical object or circumstance, but only in our mind is it "bad traffic." And this traffic isn't one amorphous whole, but is instead a combination of almost countless parts. And each of those parts is made up of countless parts. Dismantle the concepts, piece by piece — like taking apart a car so that all that remains are metal, wires, tires, plastic, upholstery, fluids — and you dismantle your disturbing emotions as well.

Here's a different, simpler travel example: One time I was flying back from Europe, and I remember feeling anxious about being trapped in a cramped "capsule" for ten hours — in fact, I'd booked a special economy section that promised six inches of extra leg room, but I doubted this would be enough. I was on the aisle, and a gentleman came to sit in the vacant window seat next to me. He was about six feet four inches tall, and as he settled into his seat, he commented, "Isn't this extra leg room great! I'm going to get a lot of sleep on this flight!"

Same flight, same size cabin. Yet despite the fact that he was nine inches taller than me, he was on a completely different inner flight! Only in my reality was the cabin "cramped." I did feel a little embarrassed, and this put my complaining mind in check. Not only had I made the mistake of treating the cramped cabin as some independent entity existing separately from my own perceptions, but I had "created" the cramped cabin to begin with. In my agitation and anxiety over what I anticipated on this flight, I had defined my need for "space" in such a way that the only thing I would experience was "cramped-ness."

It is like if you take an ugly car and lay out all of the pieces: Where is the "ugliness"? In the airplane, where is the "cramped-ness" once my attachment to "my space" disappears? As my fellow traveler demonstrated, the definition of "my space" is fluid and changeable, and it doesn't have any inherent relation to one's size or the space you're occupying. It has to do with your expectations and projections.

With so many factors affecting our perception of the present moment, how often are we really in touch with what is going on in our universe and with others? And yet, there are times when we are truly close to reality. We do feel connected to others, and we do experience the beauty of life and our humanity. We release our concepts and disturbing emotions and appreciate life as it is right now. But these experiences are too few and far between. Were we to live for ninety years, our time spent in the beauty of living our life fully, presently, truly, would amount to just a few days. We can do better. In fact, we are entitled to do better. We have this freedom and gift that we are not using; it's ours, but sometimes we don't even know we have it. It is like we are in jail and just outside is freedom and beauty. We keep looking for a means to escape when the key to our cell door is pinned to the back of our shirt.

EXERCISE: DECONSTRUCTING TRAFFIC

The next time you are in bad traffic, notice that you have labeled your situation "being in bad traffic," and notice whatever disturbing emotions you may be feeling: agitation, frustration, or just resignation. See your concept and emotions like objects, and then start to take them apart.

First, appreciate how solid and real the object seems. It is whole and complete, a single entity: bad traffic.

Next, look more closely. What are all the pieces and parts it contains? How many cars are there, and what kind? What colors are the cars, and what are the pieces that make up each automobile? Regard the bumpers, tires, sunroofs, chrome, and seats in themselves.

Next, where are you? Notice your total environment: What is and is not part of the "traffic"? What is the roadway like — the median, the lampposts, the sidewalks, the surrounding foliage and buildings?

Finally, become aware of the mass of people who are involved: the drivers and passengers; perhaps road workers, police officers, or medical personnel. Are there people "outside" of the traffic: walking by or in their home? What might their experience be? Each person has their own conception of the world you're sharing in this moment, and all these perceptions are equally valid.

Continue in this way, breaking everything down into smaller interconnected parts until you have a kind of epiphany: keep going until your concept of "bad traffic" that has been layered upon all these parts has disappeared entirely and been replaced with the infinite collection of parts and perceptions that is the present moment. Feel this sense of shared projection. Sense that it is inaccurate. Pay attention to the effects this shift in perspective has upon your mental experience and well-being.

This exercise can be practiced in any setting, but since we all have "extra" time in traffic, we might as well put it to good use! In this way, we learn to distinguish between *what we see* and *how we perceive*. We can discern the interdependent nature of the world and our minds and emotions, and we can learn how to deconstruct our reality right before our eyes. This is a liberating, freeing experience. How can we get uptight about "bad" traffic when we know that it arises only inside our mind?

EXERCISE: BAD COMMUTE

Do this exercise on a busy day. You want a certain degree of challenge and irritation. You will be deliberately treating yourself as a laboratory experiment.

As you get in your car to commute to work or to run errands, pause before turning on the ignition. Get in touch with your mindset. What is your mental picture of what you hope to accomplish and your subtle expectation of how things will go for you? Have you got a time constraint?

Have you got a certain number of tasks to fulfill? What conflict or problem might arise if something goes wrong? Or are you excited about something good that might happen? Are you meeting a friend for lunch? Are you excited, nervous, lackadaisical?

Next, start driving, and deliberately make your commute worse. Try to get a series of red lights or take a more crowded route. Let others merge ahead of you. What happens to your state of mind? Don't avoid "bad traffic," or try to escape it; embrace it. Make your commute as difficult and time-consuming and irritating as possible. Fit yourself in behind the slowest driver; *become* the slowest driver (safely). Thank everyone who gets in your way or stops you, forcing you to wait: they are helping you create the worst commute you can.

When you get to your destination, turn off your ignition and assess yourself. Do not rush to your meeting or errand, but sit for two minutes and reflect. Was it hard to let go of your typical anxieties and frustrations? Or, by seeking "bad traffic," did your experience of it become something else? Was it "fun" to play this game? Did "thanking" your traffic problems change your experience of them? Could you try this practice anytime you're "in a hurry"?

In other words, can you learn to subvert your own expectations and embrace your "problems" every day, every week, for *your whole life*?

This exercise is designed to push your mental muscles a little further. Just like when you start to work out at a gym, having not really exercised much in your life, you start to push yourself to get in better shape. At first, you take it easy on the treadmill, and then after a period of time, you look forward to making the settings more challenging.

CHAPTER SIX

Searching for Happily Ever After

I n his Second Noble Truth, the Buddha put his finger on an ironic fact of life: our very desire for happiness is what causes us to be unhappy. We might call this a "hard truth," for our desires represent, almost by definition, those things we want and are least eager to give up. And on its face, this principle is confusing. How in the world could striving for and getting what we want make us unhappy? And how exactly does the Third Noble Truth work, that by *giving up* the struggle for what we want, we'll achieve *lasting* happiness? Yet all the Buddhist masters are unwavering on this point. As the Tibetan Buddhist saint Milarepa put it: "All worldly pursuits have but one unavoidable and inevitable end, which is sorrow."

This chapter will cast light on that seemingly innocuous yet endlessly harmful thing called desire. We endlessly pursue any number of supposedly good, positive things throughout the course of our lives: education, wealth, status, sexual pleasure, love, friendship, achievement. At times we succeed; we fulfill our desires and feel satisfaction, happiness, and even euphoria. But inevitably, and much more quickly than we'd like, the moment passes, the situation changes, the feelings ebb. Our pleasures are extremely short-lived and unsustainable.

The changeable, transient, ephemeral nature of life eventually undermines all our efforts and successes. The things we achieve — a college education, a spouse, a house, a new car — eventually decay, break apart, lose their luster, or simply end. And each thing that desire leads us to acquire brings with it its own set of problems. Even at its best, pursuing our desires becomes an emotional roller-coaster of struggle, momentary elation, and then mourning, as what we've achieved fades away.

But pursuing desire also sometimes becomes a way we avoid the uncomfortable truth of impermanence. We know, even if we rarely think about it, that dissolution, aging, and death await us all. And if the thought of this makes us so uncomfortable we can't bear to contemplate it, or if we don't even see the value of reflecting upon it to begin with, then our only choice is to willfully ignore or avoid these certainties. When we pursue pleasures and desires with this agenda, then they are really only unconscious, unfettered, unquestioned, unchallenged distractions. These kinds of distractions, whatever their forms, are just types of mental "escape." When this happens, we can say that desire is not the problem as much as ignorance — ignorance of the value and skill of confronting our vulnerabilities. Thus, in all these ways, desire left to its own devices is a bit like leaving a raccoon alone in your house. Eventually it will create a mess and wreak havoc.

FOREVER IS NOT WHAT IT USED TO BE

Everything changes, everything dies. It's that simple. As we saw in the last chapter, we tend to forget this truth; we prefer to think of things, people, and ourselves as fixed entities. But it doesn't take much to see that this is wrong. Our bodies grow older every day; the atoms in our limbs are constantly changing without even a moment of stagnation. The cells of our body wholly replace themselves over the course of our life. The physical world is defined by its continual cycles of birth, growth, decay, and evolution.

But our minds are constantly changing as well. Our emotions are fleeting and malleable. The perceptions of our senses shift. Our mind and mood can change on a dime. What this means is that change is constant, even when change is so slow or subtle our senses do not register it. In fact, we are conditioned to *not* see subtle changes and to gloss over differences. The constancy and continual chatter of our mind deceive us. Yet, one day, we look in the mirror and we see that we are older, and we realize that our attitudes and sensibilities are not the same as when we were ten, or twenty, or thirty.

We look at the mountains and the oceans and the sun and think: They are solid, unchanging, eternal. They have always been like that and will always remain. But they won't. They are fluid and impermanent. This mystery is the very essence of life and beauty and reality. We cannot cling and hold on to the water flowing in a stream. We can enjoy the moving water, the colors, the patterns, the movement of the ripples. But if we try to grasp or hold on to the water, our efforts will be fruitless.

And so it is with all that flows through our mind and our perceptions. Our thoughts, our sorrows, our happiness — everything is like moving water. Nothing remains static. This is what Buddhists mean when they say we must let go of desire. If we can enjoy and appreciate this flow, without holding on to what we want or running from what we don't, we will live in a true state of balance, fulfillment, and serenity.

PLEASURE VERSUS HAPPINESS

Another ingrained misconception is that pleasure and happiness are synonymous. *They are not.* When we do not understand the difference between pleasure and mental well-being, we mistakenly believe that the sensations and feelings of a pleasurable experience will lead to or produce contentment. This is another way desire wreaks havoc. The mental quality that accompanies pleasure is contradictory to a state of balance and peace. Frequently, we pursue pleasures for the "adrenaline rush" they provide: it's the thrill of buying something new, drinking and dancing in a nightclub, working out in the gym, or having sex. As we know too well, the rush of physical pleasure fades quickly and must be fed continually.

Eating is an excellent metaphor for this situation. We get hungry, we experience some "suffering," and we want to relieve it. So we enjoy a good steak dinner. In the moment, it's wonderful, but the amount of time we spend eating and satisfied is relatively small compared to the time we spend shopping, preparing, and cleaning up. If we've gone out to eat, we had to earn the money to pay for our meal. Perhaps we don't mind if the meal is truly excellent, but the next day, we must do it again. And the day after that, and so on. And on balance, with all the money, dishwashing, shopping, and cooking it involves over the course of our entire life: Is this the road to contentment? If one meal, one pleasure, were enough to achieve lasting contentment, satisfaction, and happiness, then we could do it once and be done.

Yet the truth is, most pleasures only create the desire for more. The more we do them, the more we want them, and the more we're willing to spend, struggle, and suffer to get them. There is an inverse relationship to satisfaction. In Buddhist psychology, this desire is likened to saltwater — the more you drink, the thirstier you become. Even scientific studies have shown that, beyond a certain point, money does not bring happiness. Money may provide conditions that make life less difficult, but it does not provide emotional balance. There's substantial evidence that people who win the lottery are not happier a year after they win. Also, sadly, many lottery winners end up broke a few years later. Discontent in high-paid, high-status professions like law and medicine are rampant.

So, the drive of desire is continuous and in some ways insatiable.

We convince ourselves that we need only a few things to be happy and content. We achieve them, and then find our contentment fades and what we desired has brought us even more problems to deal with. So our suffering and displeasure are multiplied. Rather than question the impulse of desire, however, we usually only focus on the next bigger, better, more perfect thing to want. Advertisers know this all too well, and it's why there's an iPhone 3, then an iPhone 4, then an iPhone 5.... When we say, "I want," we are talking about pursuing pleasure. If we quietly investigate our motives for the actions we take, we will see that nearly every action we engage in is driven by either the desire for pleasure or the desire to be free from irritation. As long as desire runs the show, desire runs us. And as long as we are not in control, we are not free and can't be content.

PURSUING THE GOOD LIFE

Buddhists often say that, to some degree, desire isn't actually the problem. Our "problem," what makes desires destructive, is that we cling to or become attached to what we desire. For example, parents desire to provide a good life for their children. That is a normal, and worthy, desire. That is a desire rooted in caring, compassion, and love.

But problems arise depending on how fixed our ideas are, or how "attached" we are to our particular vision of what a "good life" means. Is it a certain lifestyle or income, and is our role to provide that for our family? If so, then if something gets in the way of our earning enough to achieve this lifestyle, we will suffer. If one's identity is attached or "stuck" to a particular role, and this forms one's definition of a "good parent," then disappointment, depression, anger, and shame will arise if we can't live up to it. Remember, everything in life is changing, impermanent. People lose their jobs all the time. There are all sorts of things that can, and will, happen to threaten one's career or impact one's lifestyle. Particularly for men, who have been so socialized to identify as the primary breadwinner, losing a job or not maintaining a certain income can result in severe depression and despondency.

But also consider: What if our children define a "good life" differently? What if they resent the hours that we work? What if they reject the lifestyle we provide for them and ask for something else instead? If we are rigidly fixed on and attached to our vision of what "providing a good life" means, then we may become resentful ourselves. Our identity as a "good parent" may feel threatened by our very children. Then, what started as a healthy, compassionate desire could turn into a toxic emotional battle over whose definition (really, whose label or projection) is "right" and "wrong." In fact, this is one reason to regard our disturbing emotions as "helpful": if we find ourselves angry when we meant to be loving, we can be certain that we have become self-defeatingly attached to our desires. If we can recognize disturbing emotions as "red flags" when they arise, we can learn to acknowledge, confront, and transform those desires, and the accompanying beliefs, opinions, and assumptions that lead to suffering.

Or consider a simpler example, like a Saturday morning ritual of going out to breakfast. Desire gets the whole thing moving. First, how ingrained is this ritual, and what is its real purpose? Let's say we have become "attached" to eating at one particular favorite restaurant, and that our family anticipates that this is our one big moment to be "a family" each week. To appreciate how desire and attachment work, we have to recognize how much energy and investment there is in fulfilling our desire. This is important because the degree to which we are invested, or attached, will be the degree to which we become disappointed, agitated, or angry when something does not happen according to our plans and expectations.

So, we head to the restaurant and see there is a long line of people; the wait for a table will be over an hour. How do we respond? Do we get annoyed, and decide to wait despite our irritation, perhaps blaming our kids for dragging their feet and not getting out the door sooner? Do we easily let our favorite restaurant go, and head to a different one where there is no wait (but not nearly as good of a menu)? Or do we patiently wait for a table, enjoying the morning sun and each other's company? We desire things to be a certain way, and our reactions show us how attached we are to them being that way. If we get "stuck," and can only be happy if things are exactly the way we desire them, then we are unable to "go with the flow."

We have waited for our table, and finally sit down. But the restaurant is packed, and the wait staff is overwhelmed. We desire a cup of coffee, but no one brings the pot. We try to wave down waiters and servers, but it's fifteen minutes before anyone fills our cup. We feel victimized and agitated; the coffee doesn't soothe our nerves, and our "favorite" restaurant is, on this day, a huge disappointment. Further, no one in our family is happy; we survived the wait okay, but now our relaxing, enjoyable Saturday morning ritual is spinning out of control. The kids are hungry. Everyone is cranky, and when the food arrives, everyone finds something to complain about. Then, before you're done, the bill arrives too soon and you feel rushed out the door. Is this okay? If everyone is stuck, attached to their desires, then a black cloud may hang over the rest of the day, and maybe even damage the future of this family ritual. If everyone can let go of attachment, of expectations, then the "pain" of the experience will leave quickly: you will laugh about it on the car ride home, and maybe you'll make up for it by doing something else, and you'll satisfy your desire for loving "family time" in a different way. Everyone will have a positive, or at least not negative, experience of the event, thus insuring that in the future the family won't look back on this time as one of those negative, dysfunctional family stories.

It is also easy to see how fulfilling our desires leads to problems. Our attachment to certain pleasures can easily career out of control. A news program once showcased the "superhuman" feats of several extraordinary individuals. The story that particularly intrigued me was of a guy who started running and now almost literally can't stop. He loved the feeling that running offered him, particularly the spike in endorphins he felt when he pushed his body through different levels of pain. Often he would run twenty or more miles in the morning and another ten before retiring to bed. On the show, he spoke about his recent achievement, an achievement he likened to a state of nirvana. He had just run fifty marathons in fifty days in all fifty of the United States. My reaction? I felt incredibly sad for this guy. He was seeking the constant flood of endorphins to keep him happy, but he had to continually run, and push his limits, to do so. He was an adrenaline junkie, and I wondered, what would he do next? Start running twenty-four hours a day? Still, in less extreme ways, we can recognize this same dynamic in all our lives. I have friends who get cranky when they miss working out for a single day. We become attached to our pleasures, and seek them more and more, and become less and less patient with our "downtime" in between experiences. We accept that more fulfillment of desire equals more happiness. It's a flawed design.

In 1984 my spiritual mentor, Lama Yeshe, who was truly a father figure for me, became gravely ill. He had had a heart condition for many years. When he was first diagnosed eight years earlier, he was given just a few months to live. Though he soon recovered enough to live a very full, rich life, by the time I was caring for him in India, he was quite ill with nausea, chest pains, dizziness, and discomfort. And yet despite his physical condition — and despite the fact that he was in the midst of creating an international organization that would grow into over 160 projects, centers, and institutions to better the world — he would say to me, with a look of complete sincerity, "I'm satisfied. I tried my best. I have no regrets." This was his way of saying, "I'm satisfied with the way things are. I have no attachment. I can die at any time." He knew that throughout his adult life he had put his best efforts into what he was trying to achieve. Lama had power over his intentions, and he knew that his motivations were as pure as he could make them. Otherwise, he let go of the results he could not control. And he did so guilt-free.

CASE EXAMPLE: INSATIABLE PETER

My clients often come to me complaining of discontent that stems from mindless questing. One client, an executive named Peter, was a darling of Silicon Valley. He moved up through the ranks of a large technology company, eventually running a division of twenty-five thousand people before he was made CEO of a newer technology start-up. Then that company was soon sold for several billion dollars, and this meant Peter now had more money than many towns. Yet he wanted more. I asked him several times, "How much is enough?" His answer: when he had $400 million and could afford his own plane.

Unfortunately, his great ambition prevented him from noticing that the rest of his life was falling apart around him. He and his wife of two decades divorced. His three children became estranged from him. His son in a fit of rage took a hammer to Peter's $70,000 Lexus and broke all the windows. In short, Peter was not a happy man. Wealthy, yes. Happy and content? No. I would talk to Peter about his philosophy of life. I believe everyone has a philosophy, though they may not think about it in this way. Peter's philosophy was that he "could have it all." One had to set one's goals high, he would say, and life wasn't worth living if one was not ambitious. However, Peter had a "problem": his mental state (not to mention his life) was in constant chaos. He lived a frenetic lifestyle in which just about every minute of every day he was pursuing something. No attainment can be enough when you believe you can have everything, and so he was addicted to always seeking. He buzzed constantly with the need to achieve more and more, and he couldn't understand why this was making him increasingly and perpetually discontent.

Peter didn't like it when I said that the "problem" was his philosophy. Peter's narrative of achievement and its importance for his happiness and the fulfillment of his life — his labels and projections — were the source of his dissatisfaction. Yet Peter, like most of us, felt threatened by the prospect of letting go of his philosophy. This is what gave his life purpose, and he was, understandably, strongly attached to it. Without it, would his life suddenly become empty and meaningless? It is scary to question one's sense of meaning. Even a small crack can leave a person reeling, particularly when it throws into question a habitual life-pattern. In Peter's case, over time and with a sense of curiosity, he saw the logic of what I described, and he agreed that he had to change his ideas. He took up the challenge, even though he proceeded slowly and cautiously.

Many people, particularly when discussing the pitfalls of sensory pleasures and materialism, think that the antidote is to give up all their possessions, move to a mountain hermitage, and live off the land. To "let go" of these desires, they think they now have to become a monk or nun and live a life of stark simplicity. In itself, such a radical conversion is highly suspect; it can rarely be sustained, and the person is most likely missing the point. The "renunciation" is in the mind, first and foremost. Many people take on an outer appearance of simplicity — they give away their stuff — but inwardly they make no change at all to their concepts. Their new lifestyle is a way to "deny" themselves, and in this way they are still at the mercy of their desires; they are no closer to contentment for having "given up" their lifestyle. Trading your BMW for a bicycle does not necessarily deepen your mental quietude and lessen the habit of desire. It might help for a moment, just as satisfying any desire feels good for a little while, but pretty soon you just redirect your habitual patterns of desire and attachment to your new lifestyle. Thus, the heart of mind training and of Buddhist psychology is to recognize disturbing emotions as the "problem" we need to fix, and these arise and are solved only within our mind. If we can do this, we will never again be confused by desire's outward appearances.

NO! NO! A THOUSAND TIMES, NO!

"I want this. I don't want that." These statements play constantly, 24/7, in our heads. Even when we brush our teeth, we are engaged in wanting one thing, clean teeth, and avoiding something else, dirty teeth and all that comes with them. In other words, aversion is just another form of desire. It is desire in reverse, the same impulse but in its opposite form. All day long we swing between wanting and avoiding, running toward certain experiences and away from others. This is another way to understand why "renouncing" things doesn't necessarily solve the problem of desire in our mind: "avoiding" material pleasures is merely the opposite expression of "wanting" them. It is often, in fact, the wanting of something else.

Clients come in for therapy wishing to be free of a painful or distressing mood or mental state. They are suffering and want it to stop. In essence, what Buddhism says, and what mind training teaches, is that suffering can be stopped, but only internally. Future suffering can be stopped only by continually refraining from creating in this moment the causes of our future suffering. And present suffering can be alleviated if we are unattached to what we want. If we are "attached" to what we want, this causes suffering; if we are "attached" to avoiding what we don't want, this causes suffering. And as soon as we think we have it all figured out, life will throw us a curveball, shifting and changing and challenging our concepts and labels. As we experience disturbing emotions because of changing circumstances, we learn to cope with and relate differently to these emotions. We disengage from our habitual relationship with them, and thus suffering ceases and we experience more contentment. We experience increasing contentment not by doing all we can to avoid suffering, but by meeting suffering head on when it occurs and transforming it. In the end, "avoiding" suffering is no more successful than pursuing pleasures to "escape" it.

Typically, among therapy clients, the suffering and unwanted emotions have arisen in their relationships with others. Their partner, their child, their colleague, or their friend is treating them in a way they do not like. The other person, to some degree, is "hurting" or "upsetting" them, or the client wants something from the other person they are not providing. These two things — seeking to avoid someone else's hurtful actions or desiring more affection or understanding — are not so different. Both bring up unwanted, dissatisfying emotions, and they are often intertwined. The client's relationships are bringing up feelings of hurt, abandonment, upset, or sadness, and so they feel unfulfilled. Not surprisingly, the client usually wants a range of things to change to create a more "ideal" relationship. The key, however, to improving their own mental well-being is to let go of their "ideal," or how they want the other person to "be" or what they want the other person to do.

As I've said before, this is not to suggest that we "accept" an abusive or hurtful relationship. When someone deliberately tries to harm us, they are fully accountable for their actions; the same is true if we harm others. Avoiding a person who is hurting us, however, is an entirely different thing than avoiding our own disturbing emotions, and this is the focus of mind training. Ultimately, whatever happens in life, how we respond is our responsibility. We take responsibility for our own happiness by getting control of our mind. Or, put differently, we increase our happiness by understanding how our mind works and learning to recognize when aversion and attachment are running the show.

FALLING IN LOVE WITH LOVE

In modern culture, romantic love is often presented as essential for creating a meaningful, satisfying life. Movies, books, and media exalt and cherish "falling in love" as a kind of miracle of happiness. As the fairytale goes, if we can only "find our soul mate," then our life will end "happily ever after." Desire for this wonderful experience is the most destructive arrow in Cupid's quiver: the notion that our happiness resides in someone else.

Little wonder that love stories in movies and books typically end at the altar, the loving couple glowing in their newly created "oneness." What happens next? Ask any married couple. Each person changes, moment by moment, day by day, and each person encounters the full complexity of the other's moods, emotions, feelings, and attitudes. We discover our "prince" still has plenty of frog left in him. Plus, nothing lasts forever, and that includes the mind-state of "being in love" that carries couples through their initial romance. And so, year after year, clients come into my practice disturbed by "not loving their partner anymore."

At the risk of sounding like a negative curmudgeon, I would say that their problem is that either the person never truly "loved" their partner to begin with or they are confusing desire with love. I'm as much of a sucker for romantic love stories as anyone, but we need to recognize that "romance" is a story. It is a creation of our mind, not a reflection of reality. It is a cultural narrative that we should question and treat with suspicion as it applies to our own life and emotional well-being. We risk making tragic errors if we don't.

"Healthy love" is the warm cherishing of another person without expectation and clinging. This love "accepts" all aspects of another person and "requires" nothing from them. This love is something we create in our own heart and give as our gift, freely, willingly. With a compassionate, open heart, we truly, sincerely, authentically want the best for the other person: the best seat in the restaurant, the best of ourselves, the best job, the most fulfilling life they can have. We create this contentment in order to share it; we don't depend on the other person in order to feel it. This "unselfish" love doesn't need the other person's happiness in order to exist, but it knows that when we increase someone else's happiness, everyone's happiness, satisfaction, and contentment multiply exponentially. Love is an essential part of life. It is the expression of inner happiness and contentment.

But here's the deal: We do experience authentic happiness in the presence of another, but then we almost immediately cling to the feeling and believe we "need" the other to feel it. We don't want to lose the feeling. We desire authentic, healthy love, and in our confusion, pursue it wrong-headedly. Authentic, "unselfish" love changes the moment we try to cling to and possess it. The moment of experiencing authentic love quickly gets replaced by self-centered thoughts like, "Is she going to just use me?" "Am I going to get back what I'm putting into this?" "Maybe I'm being taken for a fool." Pure love and attachment are mutually exclusive. One cannot exist in the presence of the other, just as a room cannot be both light and dark at the same time.

Thus, my suggestion to clients who say they "do not love their partner anymore" is to look within themselves first. They must confront the confusions and disturbing emotions of their desires in order to "find" their ability to love authentically again. We need to become familiar with how the mind works. When we experience authentic love, we feel so good we want to freeze the moment. Clinging takes over. This dynamic is the same as with any other desire or pleasure; we come to feel we need a good meal, a certain income, in order to be happy, content, or satisfied. When it comes to another person, our desire can similarly "objectify" them; they become a "thing" we selfishly require. Naturally, we have loving relationships with our partners, our parents, our children, and so on, and these relationships are not possessed wholly by selfishness. But in all of our relationships there tends to be an element of "What's in it for me?" If any previously loving and fulfilling relationship comes to feel harmful, toxic, unhealthy, or simply unsatisfying, then we benefit the relationship, ourselves, and the other person by examining our attitudes and becoming aware of our desires, our wants, our needs, and our demands.

Or, oftentimes, we "fall in love" only with our projections and desires, and we never really see the other person as they are to begin with. This type of "love" isn't the authentic, unselfish love described above; it is only attachment to the object of our desire. Like any projection, this type of conventional "love" cannot survive in the face of the complex reality of another person. For instance, consider the story of Rachel and Stu. When they came to see me, they would sit on my couch cuddling, caressing, and exchanging affectionate looks. Stu had expressed a number of times how he had become instantly attracted to Rachel and that he made it his project to woo her. Now, newly married, they were in therapy because they would find themselves arguing, sometimes violently. They were confused and distraught. Why were they simultaneously affectionate and angry with each other?

What we discovered was that they had each fallen in love with an illusion of the other — one that had blinded them to true questions of compatibility. They exemplified the "opposites attract" romantic love story: Rachel was self-awarely attractive and Stu was studiously ordinary. Rachel was in her early twenties, while Stu was in his late thirties. He was an engineer; she was into marketing and sales. She was athletic; he was a couch potato. She was vibrant and extroverted; he was somewhat depressed and a loner.

In the flush of romance, each saw in the other only the qualities they wanted to see, which to some degree were projections of qualities they thought might be helpful in balancing themselves. Rachel and Stu "completed" each other, and they either ignored any undesirable qualities or excused them as cute and quirky. The desire for romance itself is one of our most powerful, and it blinds us in all sorts of ways. Once the "romance" is over, reality intrudes, like water from a rainstorm leaking through a small hole in the roof. In Stu and Rachel's case, their conflicts ran deeper than their attractions. Stu lost his job, their marriage fell apart, and Rachel moved back to her native Australia with their two children — without Stu.

EXERCISE: WHERE DID I COME FROM?

Set aside time for an extended reflection. When you're ready, start by thinking of yourself now, in this moment. What is it that got you here? Describe this: "I am here because..." Now go back to this morning, before you ate breakfast: What was it that created the "I" at that time? Then go back to yesterday, at the end of the day, when you felt tired: What was it that got your "I" there? Who was that tired "I"? How was it created and what was its "support system" or scaffolding? Look at him or her. Now go back to yourself as a child. Think of a time in your childhood; really feel it and see it in your mind. What were the conditions that created that "I" experience? Now go back to where you came from — your parents, your birth. Get a sense of the "I" who experienced the birth. After staying in this experience for a few minutes, return to the present moment. Ask yourself again: Where did this present "I" come from? Can you list or see all the contributing factors that create your present experience, your present "I"? When doing this exercise, you should feel the "I" is a dependent entity, something created from multiple elements. As a result, the sovereign attitude and seemingly independent stature of your "I" should be weakened.

CHAPTER SEVEN

Who Do You Think You Are?

Buddhist thought proposes that we all suffer from a misperception of reality. Our "misleading mind" treats the thoughts,
emotions, and concepts that it creates (and which exist *only* in our
mind) as real, thus missing what is true and real in our experiences
of life. This includes our concept of self, or the self-referential "I"
at the heart of every emotion or desire, such as when we say, "I
feel…" or "I want…" In other words, Buddhist thought maintains
that our everyday sense of self is mistaken, and until we realize this,
we won't be able to truly get free of all the disturbing emotions that
arise within us.

Typically, this is one of the most difficult ideas for people to
understand and accept. We are naturally attached to our own identity. The "truth" that is perceived by our senses and reflected in our
mind is that there must be an independent, individual "self" who
perceives and experiences everything, and we believe this is the
unique person we have grown to become: one with a past, likes and
dislikes, talents and weaknesses, hopes and goals, and all the other
things we mean when we refer to our "personality." Many modern

people are perplexed and threatened by the Buddhist notion that this self is "false." Without that, then who are we? What are we? Let me be 100 percent clear: It is not that we don't exist or that there is no self or identity. The central theme being presented here is that *the self does not exist in the way it appears, in the way we believe it to exist.*

In fact, showing how our perceived sense of self is like a mirage, and often a self-defeating one, is relatively easy. It's remembering, maintaining, and living the truth of this that's hard. Ultimately, in Buddhist thought, understanding or perceiving how the self appears incorrectly is a primary goal. It is the actualization of wisdom, and wisdom is the key antidote to our disturbing emotions and unhealthy mind. Fully actualizing this wisdom, in which all falsehoods fall away, is generally what is meant by the spiritual pursuit of "enlightenment," but to me this is no different than, and could be considered a euphemism for, "mental health."

In any case, the main purpose of this chapter is to show how the idea of a "false sense of self" follows logically from everything we've discussed so far, and to show how, in practice, this false self gets us into trouble more often than not. Understanding this fundamental function of ignorance is the deepest, most profound of methods leading to mental health and balance. Our mistaken sense of identity is a habitual, primary contributor to our mental dissatisfaction and our limited level of happiness, and we serve ourselves best when we learn to treat it with increasing skepticism.

CASE EXAMPLE: EMERGING EMILY

Emily was one of my very first clients. She started seeing me when I was still an intern and has continued to see me off and on until the present time. For the first half of our therapeutic work, she sought counseling primarily to help her be a better single mother for her two sons. However, after her sons reached young adulthood, the therapeutic focus shifted to investigating her relationships with men. She tended to seek men who would treat her poorly; they were often alcoholics or substance abusers who eventually took her for granted. She understood herself to be "codependent" in the classic sense, as someone who was caretaking of another person at the expense of her own well-being.

Emily is an excellent example of how our constructed sense of self — our perception of who we are — can undermine our own happiness, as well as of how transforming that self-destructive "version" of reality can lead us to make better choices and increase our happiness. Eventually, Emily became involved with a man who was not a substance abuser nor had any history of alcohol or drug problems. But their otherwise loving relationship did contain one minor problem — he was married. His relationship with his wife, he told Emily, was on the skids, and they were preparing to separate and divorce. Emily took him at his word, and as time went on, she developed a strong dependence upon his company and affection. For two years their relationship continued in this vein: him on the verge of leaving his wife, Emily waiting in the wings while enjoying his limited companionship. Finally, Emily began to feel hurt, used, taken for granted, and manipulated, in similar ways as in her previous relationships. She knew she should end things, but the alternative, being alone without a man while her own two boys were moving out and on with their lives, appeared far worse. Her decision-making was clouded by disturbing emotions of fear, and this was leading her to cling to a self-destructive relationship under a mistaken belief that it offered her only source of safety and comfort.

Why would she do this? In truth, Emily's root problem was her attachment to a sense of self that believed it would be happy and complete if she had a man, any man, in her life. Her sense of identity just did not fit without a man. This understanding of self made her behavior, in her mind, seem logical, and even necessary or justified. We would talk frequently about this: Who was this "Emily" who was not entitled to a loving relationship with a man? Where did this "I" come from? How did it come to dominate her life and convince her to believe in this version of "Emily"? At one point Emily asked me, "Do you think it's the abuse I suffered as a young girl?" I was taken aback. "Abuse? What abuse?" I asked. This had never come up before. I knew Emily's father had abandoned the family when she was quite young, and we discussed this as a source of her mindset. Afterward, her mother had become involved with their priest, who eventually left the church to pursue their relationship. However, I didn't know that the priest had sexually abused Emily and her sister before he got romantically involved with their mother, nor that the abuse continued once he moved into their home.

Here we had finally found a source of the fear and pain that was confusing Emily's mind when it came to men. Like many abuse survivors, Emily had integrated into her identity her relationship with her abuser. In other words, she had come to accept the terms of the abusive relationship: at a young, vulnerable age, she came to believe she was inherently unworthy of love and respect, and submitting to a male's authority, giving up her own will and control, was the "price" for experiencing any affection at all. Since then, her self-worth had remained so low that she didn't believe she "deserved" anything more. It was this "I" that would take the steering wheel whenever she entered into a relationship with a man.

Up until this moment, Emily thought that these emotions, this role she took in relationships, was her. However, once we'd labeled this "I" and identified its source, Emily discovered that this "I" was just one of several identities that inhabited her psyche. She began to see this "I" as a constructed entity, a collection of opinions, projections, and disturbing emotions, rather than something that was absolute. This "I" was more like a persona that had been reinforced so many times throughout her life that it had come to seem "real" — as if Emily had cast herself as a character in a play, and eventually she had played that character so many times she naturally felt it was "her." Once she understood this process of creating a persona, it began to have less control over her. Emily discovered she could substitute other roles that were more functional, helpful, and healthy. She began to focus more upon these healthier identities, reinforcing them instead, and thus they became more dominant. However, the very process of recognizing the constructed nature of identity, and realizing she could decide who (or how) to be, helped illuminate the fundamental "trick" of her mind. Her previous unhealthy identity of "being no good" was a lie, but then no "self," no matter how positive and helpful it seems, is entirely "true" or "real" either. Why is this distinction important? Because now, if she finds herself "attached" to an identity that becomes self-defeating, she knows she can change it. She can gain some measure of control over a process that usually controls us and develop more healthy, productive attitudes. The person of "Emily" is only a story or narrative her mind creates as a way to make sense of her experience.

This revelatory process about the nature of our false self is akin to the little dog Toto pulling back the curtain to reveal the machinations of the Wizard in the *Wizard of Oz*. Throughout the Land of Oz, the Wizard was dominant, all-powerful, and authoritative, and everyone deferred to him. This is like our ego, telling us what to do and convincing us that it alone is wise and knows all. Then, one day, we get fed up and tired of being sent on wild goose chases, and we discover that the big Wizard is only a rather small, insecure, and powerless old man shouting into a microphone. It is all a ruse. The Wizard dominated for his own benefit; Dorothy never needed him to get her "home." Our personal Wizard might be the internalized voice of an abuser; it might be the internalized voice of our parents, or of society, or of our profession. The Wizard is not us, however, and we don't actually need him in the driver's seat. Invariably, getting "home" and overcoming our self-destructive tendencies require us only to be brave enough to pull back the curtain and reveal our own false sense of self.

A PORTRAIT OF THE FALSE SELF

Like Emily, we all maintain a false sense of self that we believe to be real. We need to confront and question this belief, since as we will see, the self, or identity, we hold as true and solid is really something that is merely projected upon our minds and bodies. It is a fabrication that we see, relate to, and engage with as something concrete, truly existent, and independent of any other conditions. But it is a phantom, of sorts. When we relate to this phantom as real, we do not see our identity the way it actually exists, and this causes ourselves unending confusion. Buddhist psychology says that "there is *someone* there; otherwise there would be no experiencer of experiences." There is an experiencer; it's just that the experiencer does not exist in the manner we think.

As Descartes said, "I think, therefore I am," and Buddhist psychology does not disagree. Perception indicates a "self"; indeed, perceptions are self-created and are therefore, as we've discussed, limited. The more important and useful question is: What is the nature of subjectivity? In other words, this chapter poses the age-old question "Who am I?" Who is the "I" who says, "I love ice cream," or "I am mad at you and need to talk"? It is curious and revealing that we constantly refer to ourselves, our "I," and yet we don't really know the manner in which this "I" exists. Where am I? Can you point to your consciousness? Am "I" my physical body: my nose, my face, my leg, my brain? However, doesn't the self or "I" survive even when we lose an arm or leg or eye?

Am "I" my mind: my emotions, thoughts, memories, and concepts? We might say, "I am my soul," but it amounts to the same thing, for what is that and where is it located? As we discussed in chapter 3, our mind is formless; it has no clear location except, generally speaking, somewhere inside and throughout our bodies. And yet, that formless consciousness cannot be identical with our body because, our body being form, the self cannot be both formless and form. These two are mutually exclusive of each other. Something cannot be space and a rock at the same time. The mind and body might be interdependent, but this does not mean they are identical. This is perhaps the first and most fundamental reason for skepticism: if, strangely enough, we cannot point definitively and specifically to *where we are*, then why are we so certain we know who we are when we point to our bodies and say, "I'm Steve," or "I'm Lisa"?

In this way, we come back to the truth that our "false" sense of self is rooted in the mistakes of perception. In chapter 3, we used the metaphor of the mirror to explain the Buddhist concept of perception: all perceptions exist like reflections in the mirror of the mind, or like clouds in the sky. Thoughts, emotions, sensations, images, and so on are "objects" that come and go like clouds; a function of the mind itself perceives them but is not identical to them. In this way, we turn the perceptions of our senses automatically into "mental stuff," like "That is a rock," "My friend hurt my feelings," and "My name is Steve." And these are all the same thing: reflections in a mirror, thoughts that float like clouds in the mind. Like the Three Umpires, our "self" is nothing until we label it (or *name* it). The "self" is something purely relative, constructed, dependent on so many factors, and yet it seems and appears as *independent*. It acts like a boss or a general of our person when, in fact, it is merely our ignorance, confusion, and habits that allow it to be in charge. To understand this — that the self appears and acts as if it were independent when it is totally dependent for its very existence upon multiple factors — is a huge part of the meaning of wisdom. However, to say there is no inherent, individual "I" is *not* to say that there is no consciousness, no mind, no experiencer or person there. Just that there is no independently existing, permanent, unchanging self as there appears to be.

Another powerful way to conceive of this is the parable of the stick. The great Indian philosopher Shantideva, who lived hundreds of years ago, noted that when someone hits us with a stick, we become angry with the person, not their weapon. "Although indeed it is the stick that hurts me, I am angry at the one who wields it, striking me. But he is driven and impelled by anger. So it is his wrath I should resent." We don't blame the stick that hits us, of course, because it is self-evident that the stick isn't in control of what it's doing, nor does the stick have any intention of its own. Literally speaking, the stick is the only thing causing us physical pain, but we know that something besides the stick is causing it to strike. This, Shantideva argues, is also true for us. When our minds become clouded with anger, we lash out. So shouldn't we be upset with the anger in another person's head that's causing them to act, rather than being angry with the person themselves? In this view, the mind of the other person is "suffering" from anger, which now controls their actions and obscures their understanding of reality, both their reality and ours. If we take this angry version of their "self" literally, as independent and thus to "blame" for hurting us, then we only join them in their delusion. Just because someone else acts irrationally doesn't mean we should.

Belief in the independent, individual, unique self is powerful, however, and not easily dislodged by logical arguments. Every day, our senses seem to reinforce that each of us is "separate" from everything else. When I walk, I walk in my shoes, not yours. When I eat, I am eating and become full, but I cannot eat and have you become full, nor vice versa. When my son is telling me about his life, it is I who is listening, not anyone else. It is I who notices the new moon at dusk and shares my wonder with my wife on our evening walk. It is our relationship with these experiences that compels us to see ourselves as the center of our own universe.

In fact, Western culture encourages us to think of ourselves as the center of our personal universe. Individualism is promoted and even exalted. And yet, in many areas of the world, the idea of "individualism" seems quite strange, if not dangerously wrong-headed. I am not an anthropologist, but I have lived many years of my life in various Eastern cultures where our concept of individualism is regarded as ill-conceived self-centeredness. In these cultures, the family, the tribe, the community, the monastery — these identities are more important than the individual self. The "center" of the universe is the community. Typically, these cultures also teach that the more one looks after oneself, the less one is actually happy. This runs directly counter to the Western "path" to happiness, which is focused almost entirely on pleasing oneself, even at the expense of others. We could say that these are both just culturally relative values and concepts, that neither is empirically valid. But we can look at both to see how well they work, and we can look at how both suggest we solve problems: in the West, an individual just has to try harder, to know themselves better, to be more successful and "happy." In Buddhism and much of the East, a person must question the concept of "individualism" itself to recover the correct path to happiness.

Further, the notion of "individualism" is historically rooted, which should make us suspicious of its presentation as an inherent "truth." When psychology developed in Europe and America during the rise of the Industrial Age, it reflected a general cultural shift to valuing the individual over the collective — the family, clan, tribe, and community. The changing nature of society due in part to technological progress, and the rise of consumerism and materialism, led people to value their individual well-being first and foremost, rather than the group's well-being. Within the writings of

Freud and other early pioneers of psychology, the whole notion of "individuation" was born; self-knowledge of one's personal history became paramount for emotional and psychological wellness. In all these and other ways, Western culture has taught that the path to happiness is "to look after number one."

The continual, unending process of imprinting only reinforces and strengthens our mistaken concept of "I." If we have accepted, as modern culture further elaborates, that there is an inherent, real "self" that makes us who we are, that there is a specific personality that is us, then we constantly "act out" this self in the world and self-perpetuate it. If we believe our perception of our "self" is real and inherent, then every perception of our five senses, and our every thought and concept, only reinforces this belief and confusion, for every thought and perception begins with "I..." These imprints never go away on their own; if they aren't actively dismantled, they only develop strength as they are reinforced through repetitive action.

So, for example:

- We lose money in a business venture, and we tell ourselves we're never going to be successful or we're no good with handling money.
- We get a poor grade in school or a poor performance review, and we tell ourselves that we're no good at certain tasks or are simply "stupid."
- We have a failed relationship, and we tell ourselves we are unlovable or "marriage is not for me."

Thus, often when we have an experience, we generalize it to a personal "trait." So, when going through various experiences, we typically reinforce an imprint of who we think we are. In a sense we could say we predispose ourselves to expect that we will live out the "story" that we think defines us, even when that story leads us into perpetual failure or self-destructive habits. It is a vicious and, if we do not intervene, unending cycle. In this way, we embrace our disturbing emotions as the defining source of our self-image because, ironically, our ignorance has tricked us into thinking that the disturbing emotions are "me," my identity. That is how we get trapped by our unhelpful and unhealthy aspects of our mind, and why our negative views of ourselves can feel so entrenched and real.

Another way we reinforce our false sense of self is through our identification with our "roles." Many people, when introducing themselves, respond by describing what they do: "I'm a consultant." "I'm a student." "I'm a truck driver." "I'm a parent, father, mother, grandmother…" Oftentimes we respond from the stance of what we think the other person wants to hear. We make a judgment call on what role best defines us, or what identity will make us look good in the other person's eyes. If we are thoughtful or teasing, we might respond by saying, "I'm a human being," but we know that's not what the other person wants to hear. Typically, they are not so interested in *who* we are but *what* we are. They want to know our story — what makes us unique or perhaps what makes us different from them — so we try to explain ourselves. And yet, while we might like to think we know ourselves like the back of our hand, in reality we know ourselves about as well as we know who invented the wheel.

How do you answer the question "Who are you?"

THE MANY ROLES OF "I"

The metaphor of acting is useful when trying to understand the multiple "I"s that exist and how they are purely relative in nature. Think of all the different roles that Tom Hanks has played in ten of his most famous movies:

1. *Splash*
2. *Forrest Gump*

3. *Saving Private Ryan*
4. *Sleepless in Seattle*
5. *Philadelphia*
6. *The Green Mile*
7. *Big*
8. *Apollo 13*
9. *Cast Away*
10. *The Da Vinci Code*

Tom Hanks knows he is not truly Captain John Miller in *Saving Private Ryan* or Forrest Gump. Yet, he is considered a great actor because he plays these roles, or identities, so well; his commitment and skill create convincing portraits of wildly diverse people that can genuinely move and inspire us. Further, playing these roles serves a useful purpose (in this case, communication and entertainment). Our multiple identities are much like the multiple roles that Hanks has played.

However, unlike Tom Hanks, who knows he is acting, we typically do not grasp the idea that we are constantly and continually playing roles. These roles, or identities, are relative and temporary and serve a purpose, but they are not who we are in an absolute sense. However, they are who we *think* we are, absolutely. Sometimes we are more self-aware of "performing" for an audience than at other times, and some roles we play are more comfortable and perhaps are more convincing and successful than others. But being a "good" actor doesn't change the fact that we are "acting" within every interaction and every relationship, even our relationship with ourselves. In our ignorance, we don't see and understand this; we are not in control of our actions. We are not in control of our life. It is as if our roles are playing us. We react to circumstances or our disturbed emotions without awareness and are unable to control, change, adjust, or stand up to whatever role we are compelled to play.

Another important distinction is that Buddhist psychology says that "Tom Hanks" is itself just a role, a designated identity, dependent upon what qualities of a person's personality are paid attention to. When Tom Hanks takes off his makeup and leaves the set, he simply shifts to the real-world roles of "Tom Hanks" the professional actor, husband, son, and so on. It is a delusion to try to identify the "real" person within or underneath one's multiple identities. We may easily recognize that "mother" and "lawyer" are limited and relative aspects of who we are, but eventually we think, "*This* is the real me," the true self beneath the facade. Yet in Buddhist thought, once we attempt to "name" a "true self," we have failed; all we have done is named, or designated, another relative persona. This idea is essential for understanding our psychology. There is no real "Tom Hanks." There is no independent, truly existing, findable, inherent "true self." And in Buddhist psychology, it's when we fail to recognize this relative nature of our self that we get into trouble in life. For instance, I could say of myself: I am a father, husband, therapist, teacher, son, impatient driver, mellow driver, good golfer, bad golfer, meditator, coach, and so on. But I am none of these concretely, permanently, solidly, independently, or absolutely, even if I do believe I exist in all those ways at certain times and places.

Let's say someone asks, "Who are you?" and you answer, "I'm a teacher." There is nothing wrong with *calling* yourself a teacher; we have to call ourselves something when others ask. Perhaps that is the best role to play for the specific interaction or moment you are in. But if you see yourself *inherently* as a teacher (as if you were "born to teach"), then you have confused yourself with one limited, and limiting, identity, and you are setting yourself up for suffering. It will be hard to impossible to act like a "teacher" in every circumstance, now and forever. More importantly, rather than choosing effectively the best way to be in any circumstance, you will always be compelled to "be" the teacher because it's your "true self." You won't act in any other way because you won't see that there's a choice; indeed, you won't see this way of being as a "role" or identity at all. By identifying a "true self," you are compelled to behave and think in that particular way. But imagine if Tom Hanks thought that he actually was Forrest Gump. He'd be considered delusional, since he wouldn't understand he was an actor. And if he thought he could play only "Forrest Gump," then he'd be considered a "bad actor." Actors get "typecast" all the time, so that they are hired to play the same type of part in every movie, and they tend to have limited careers. Thus, we become "successful" actors in our life when we learn to cultivate flexibility, awareness of roles, and control over the ones ignorance compels us to play.

I admit, it can be disconcerting to realize that there is no "inherent" self. Even after considering this idea, we will struggle against this truth. We may recognize that, throughout life, we are constantly changing and that we slip from one identity to another, unconsciously or without deliberate intent. But we try to avoid having "multiple personalities" and the seemingly "schizophrenic" quality of self this implies. We prefer to see ourselves as just one entity with one personality, and so we spend an inordinate amount of time trying to assemble one coherent, consistent, cohesive, unchanging "self." One way we do this is by cultivating our opinions, beliefs, and "ideals" — our philosophy. In a sense it is more accurate to say that these opinions, beliefs, and ideals hold on to us, for it's a reciprocal relationship. To have an identity, we need an opinion or belief; to have a belief or opinion, we need an identity. This is really what it means to say that identities are not "real," since to exist they are interdependent with, or dependent on, other things, like opinions and thoughts and beliefs.

One example is political beliefs: "All politicians are corrupt." "Government's purpose is to care for its poorest citizens." "Environmentalists are out to destroy free enterprise." These beliefs and opinions filter into so many aspects of our life, and we may take great pride in how studiously we uphold certain principles in every situation: "I always do what I promise, and never promise what I can't do." But then, what happens when we fail? What happens when, one time or several times, we overpromise and don't deliver? Or when we embrace environmental regulations in order to keep the woods behind our home from being turned into a strip mall? We have, by choice, restricted who and what we are allowed to be by rigidly abiding by a "true self" with certain beliefs and opinions and values. It is common that events will challenge us and force us to act outside of these limits. Often this can cause us to question and doubt our entire worldview, leading us to confusion, doubt, and even anger and depression at having our point of view questioned. We suffer shame, guilt, blame, or avoidance.

It is as if we believe that a different "I," or subject, arises with each set of beliefs, and we cannot abide this. We must experience continuity of self. Yet our beliefs are learned and acquired; they are not an inherent part of our identity. And since beliefs and opinions are changeable, so is any identity that's based on them. This is good news given that our changeable nature allows us to acquire more helpful beliefs and shed those that are harmful. We should be happy beliefs are so malleable. Interestingly, like the definition of a "bad actor," we generally consider those who can only hold one belief, and who treat their beliefs as inseparable from their identity, to be "close-minded" or even bigoted. We recognize when someone has gone too far and become ignorant of the need for flexibility of belief, opinion, and point of view. Thus, even though the full implications of it can be upsetting, we typically understand that, to be successful in our everyday lives, our sense of self must be seen as continuously changeable and adaptable depending upon the context we find ourselves in.

EMOTIONAL FUSION

We all, most likely, would agree that we are not our beliefs, our experiences, or our roles. We know intellectually that we are not solely any of these limited things, but there's the rub. Despite this understanding, we often behave and react otherwise. We "forget" in the heat of the moment. We live in a kind of a hallucination brought on by our emotions, which are experienced so fully and directly it's as if they take over our mind and we "fuse" our identity with them.

Look at how we talk about our emotions. Usually, we say we "are" the thing that we feel, physically or emotionally. We'll say, "I am hungry." And how funny: We're now no longer a project manager; we are hunger. We say, "Boy, am I tired!" Or, "I am relaxed after that walk." Or, "I'm mad at my boss and anxious about my job review." In the moment, we *become* anger or relaxation or anxiousness. In fact, all day long we are constantly identifying with our emotions, and we treat them as if they are the infallible barometer of our true self.

But are they? As with self-consciously named roles like "father" or "teacher," we sometimes treat emotional states of mind as permanent aspects of our self. For example, depression. When we're depressed, the feeling itself may seem unending, as if it will never go away. Of course, we know even our strongest feelings will change over time, eventually, but we may still come to believe that we are a depressive person by nature (or an angry person, or an anxious person, and so on). This quality feels like an unchanging, concrete part of ourselves, and our attitude is: I'm always going to be depressed, now and forever, because that is who I am and how I've always been. I *am* depression.

And yet, this becomes just another limited identity, the "depressed person." Further, no emotion exists out of context, without being related to or dependent on what else is going on. Certain disturbing emotions arise or are triggered by certain identities, which arise due to particular circumstances. Though our disturbing emotions are experienced directly, arising unpremeditated and instantly in reaction to events, they still remain products of a specific context. We almost never consciously choose how we react. And in fact, we can use our disturbing emotions to help us see and identify the "role" or "identity" particular situations cast us in.

For instance, take stress. We experience stress often, and it can seem diffuse and general. Yet we tend to become anxious when we fear certain consequences, and these are directly related to what we have decided to value. Say you have a deadline for a project you are working on, and you are becoming more and more stressed as the deadline approaches. Naturally, the date of the deadline is itself arbitrary; it is entirely the product of the context of your job. If your deadline is July 15, what is "July 15"? It is merely a label, and its reality as a "deadline" does not exist except as a concept, albeit a concept in many people's minds. Even the fact that it is a shared concept, a mutually agreed-upon date for the completion of work, does not make the deadline any more "real" in any inherent sense. Indeed, our whole lives are spent in just such mutually agreed-upon fictions, and yet the stress and anxiety we feel don't seem arbitrary or made up. Once we become anxious, that anxiousness feels real, and it lives inside us until we alone take control of it and transform it.

At this point, the deadline is not our problem; anxiety is our problem. We might believe the deadline caused our anxiety, but it has not. We caused our own anxiety by projecting specific beliefs, perceptions, and values onto the deadline. We need to ask ourselves: What identity of mine is affected by this deadline, and how will that role, my sense of "I," suffer if I don't meet it? Am I clinging to my reputation as a "good worker," and thus will that identity suffer if I am seen as irresponsible? Am I clinging to my identity as a competent, reliable, smart professional? If I don't get perceived by others that way, then am I the opposite: an unreliable, untrustworthy, lazy good-for-nothing? Would this hurt my career path, which provides the money, prestige, and personal satisfaction I want for myself? Perhaps all of this. My anxiety, then, is the direct result of this desire/aversion I have around a specific identity, and my attachment to one outcome, one personality. This one particular deadline is now clearly nothing compared to what I have riding on it. Little wonder that this deadline is causing me discomfort, fear, aversion, dread, and anxiety.

The disturbing emotions that arise are bedfellows of our false sense of self. Another good example is the recent experience of a client of mine, Jack.

He and his sister attended an important meeting with some financial advisors to discuss how to handle the rather large investment portfolio of Jack's ailing father. Jack related to me how frustrated and agitated he became in the meeting with the advisors. Jack explained, "My sister would not keep her mouth shut. They would ask me a question, and she would answer for me. She butted in and dominated the conversations with inane and irrelevant statements about our family. She would tell stories of family vacations we took as children, conversations my parents had with our teachers in parent-teacher conferences, how our parents didn't like traveling to Africa, and on and on. It was so unprofessional and embarrassing."

Clearly, Jack was experiencing the disturbing emotions of agitation, anger, impatience, and embarrassment. He blamed his sister and her behavior as the cause, but rather than focusing on the false identity that arose or the disturbing emotions themselves, and his discomfort at feeling them, Jack needed to ask: *Who is this "I" who was embarrassed?*

Looking at the "I" who is embarrassed is a unique, and advanced, practice of Buddhist psychology, which not only considers all emotions to be products of context, but the "I" of the perceiver as well. We assume that the experiencer of an emotion exists quite concretely, and emotions themselves are concrete and real, but the "I" that arises in relationship with the emotions does not exist the way it appears.

In Jack's case, the feeling of embarrassment is the "object" to be perceived; it's the cloud passing through the sky of his mind. Yet when Jack experiences this, he doesn't say to himself: "Jack in the identity of the effective, efficient professional is feeling embarrassed." He says, "I am embarrassed," and here is the whole crux of the problem: in the moment, we experience an emotion as the same or inseparable from the I, or the identity, of the perceiver. Upon reflection, we may say, "I have embarrassment," or "I feel embarrassed," but invariably, in that initial flash, we are, mistakenly, one with embarrassment. This feeling of unity with the emotion is the problem.

When we are nervous before seeing the dentist, our anxiety is not seen as something separate from our sense of self. We say, "I'm really nervous about getting my teeth drilled," and the internal experience is not one of a "designated" or "relative" self and nervousness. We *are* nervousness. This misconception or dynamic, and its variations, is what is in action with *all* of our problems. When we feel depressed, our self-identity becomes fused with depression. We have an extremely difficult time objectifying or depersonalizing depression. We are depression. This sense of fusion is graded, in that there are degrees of fusion. When the degree of fusion is massive, we could say we get "body and psyche snatched." We can literally see no end and no alternative to our hopelessness; in fact we become the very incarnation of hopelessness, and then it is not surprising that a depressed person will feel suicidal. Death is considered the only alternative to finding release from hopelessness and its identity of a hopeless self.

Had Jack been completely fused with the emotion of anger, he might have acted out in a similarly "pathological" way. He might have attacked his sister physically or yelled at her to stop. Instead, he told me, he gave her "that look," and she understood and stopped interrupting him and talking in the way that she was. But until Jack recognizes what identity his "I" is when it experiences, and gets taken over by, anger and embarrassment in these situations, he will always be at the mercy of his disturbing emotions. Indeed, each time it happens he will no longer be the person or role he wants to be, not because of someone else, but because he has become "lost" in a struggle with his own afflictive emotions.

CASE EXAMPLE: MY HEROINE, LOUISE

If we exercise our freedom to choose how we relate with our emotions and how much we draw our identity from them, we slowly and surely become happier and healthier people. If we choose not to let the circumstances of our life dictate "who we are" — even such seemingly inherent aspects of ourselves like our physical body, our gender, and our nationality — we allow our best selves a chance to emerge. This is why Louise — who is a younger sister of my wife, Pam — is one of my heroes. Louise is such an extraordinary example of how our identity is something we can choose. In 1973, Louise was fifteen years old and a renowned child actress in Australia. She was one of the leading characters on a hit TV drama, and on her own initiative, she had dropped out of school to pursue her love of acting.

But that year her life took a sudden detour. The family had spent Christmas a few hundred miles north of their home in Melbourne. Louise, Pam, their father, their brother, and a friend were driving back to Melbourne, and the rest of the family planned to follow later. It was the day after Christmas, or Boxing Day in Australia. The family had stopped for lunch, and when they resumed driving, the children traded seats — Dad driving, the friend in the front passenger seat, their brother and Pam on the sides in the back seat, and Louise between them, sitting in the middle. They were cruising on the two-lane country highway when, apparently, they all fell asleep. No one remembers exactly what happened, but Pam woke up to screaming and there was pandemonium everywhere. They had had a head-on collision with another car. Everyone was wearing seatbelts (which was the law in Australia, a decade before seatbelt laws were adopted in the United States), but Louise was the only one without a shoulder harness. Pam unbuckled her seat belt, got out of the car, and then collapsed. The next thing she remembers is being in the ambulance racing to the country hospital.

Because of Louise's notoriety, the newspapers covered the story on their front page. Pam suffered spinal fractures and multiple internal injuries, and her brother also had a spinal fracture; however, they were lucky because their spinal cords had not been severed. Their father had massive injuries to his face, and their friend had nothing but a scratch on her forehead. The passenger in the front seat of the other car was killed. Meanwhile, Louise suffered a broken back and her spinal cord was severed. The fifteen-year-old child actress was paralyzed from the waist down, and she would remain paralyzed that way for the rest of her life. And yet, she never missed a beat. While Pam and Louise were recuperating in the same hospital room, Louise never shed a tear or complained about her situation. Pam was in severe pain, with three broken vertebrae and massive internal injuries. Louise felt fine, except she couldn't walk. She spent her time in the hospital helping Pam feel better by cracking jokes and incessantly telling stories.

When Louise left the hospital, in the midst of what should have been typical "teenagehood," she remained upbeat. The television series wrote her back into the script by having her character involved in an accident and returning wheelchair bound. Louise continued to land popular TV roles until she gave up acting several years later. She married, gave birth to three sons, and has a thriving public relations business. While she may have given up acting, she has not "given up" in any other sense, and her passion is to provide a positive impact for others.

At one time, she was in charge of public relations for tourism for the state of Queensland. She hosted her own radio shows. She lobbied for the rights of those facing disabilities, and she was instrumental in Australia's passing some of the world's most progressive laws supporting the physically challenged. She continues to be in high demand for her motivational speeches, and she never ceases to work for those who are disadvantaged.

She is my hero for all these reasons, but also because she personally opened my eyes. When I first met Louise in the early 1980s, I had never actually known anyone who was "confined" to a wheelchair. I was tentative before our first meeting, not knowing what to expect or how I should act around her. Yet an amazing thing happened: the force of Louise's personality drove her wheelchair from my image of her. She was not "Louise in a wheelchair" because Louise never identified with her paralysis. Because of her own self-image (which didn't include her wheelchair), her ability to choose an "I" that fit her happiness with life, she allowed me to see her differently as well. "Handicapped Louise," she would explain to me, was not a fitting or a useful label. She understood that *she* was not her *condition*.

I remember many years later, Louise and I were watching a program about a recent medical discovery. Scientists were having amazing success inserting microchips in spinal cord–injury patients and creating electrical impulses that allowed some movement in the paraplegics' legs. As we watched the program, I remember becoming encouraged, and I asked Louise, "Would you consider doing this procedure once it became more credible?" I was surprised when she hesitated, then responded, "I'm not that concerned. If somebody needed it more than me, I'd let them have it." I felt my question was a bit like asking a pastry chef if she wanted a bite of my Pop-Tart.

Louise had decided a long time ago that she was not going to choose an identity, an "I," that would be defined by what she did not have or by what was lacking: the ability to walk on two legs. Thinking of herself as "paraplegic" just was not all that useful to her.

LOSE YOUR SELF, GAIN COMPASSION

We resist any effort to deconstruct our created sense of self. While it causes us problems at times, we feel familiar with our identity, and if Buddhist philosophy says that's a misperception of reality, a "false sense of self," we might respond: "What's so great about reality?"

This might be called the "ignorance is bliss" approach to life. And so long as our problems aren't too big, it's hard to argue with it. Of course, misconceiving reality, and misconceiving who we are, invariably leads to problems that seriously affect our well-being. And whatever the size of our problems, we won't attain a higher quality of life. Until we understand who we really are, we'll never effectively solve our individual problems or those in the world at large and achieve the kind of well-being and happiness that is possible. But typically, it takes problems of great seriousness before we willingly dismantle our attachment to our "self," to the identity that has served us for so long.

Yet, Louise's story exemplifies another reason to actively do so. By loosening our attachment to our individual sense of self and acknowledging that all people and things exist interdependently, we become kinder people. We become more compassionate and empathetic. As we "lose" our attachment to our belief in our inherent self, we gain a feeling of interconnectedness with all others — not only with our lover, our children, our parents, and our friends, but with all people in the world. As we realize how our false sense of self leads us to make mistakes and create our own problems, we see that that's how everyone else operates as well — and this understanding heightens our feelings of affection, kindness, and warmth. As we soften the conception of our self as concrete, solid, and independent, we soften our concept of others as having concrete, solid, independent selves, and we increase our sense of connection to the wider community and the world at large.

We will look at this more closely in the final chapter, but how does this work in practice? Say you are the manager of a business, and you are dealing with an irate customer who insists you (or your company) is "wrong." Instead of "becoming" the manager and solidly "holding your ground," you see yourself and the customer as unwilling actors in a play. Really, you are just two people meeting for a short moment in the continuum of life, and what does it matter what part you play, so long as the "problem" is solved and kindness and happiness are increased...for both of you? Perhaps the other person has a tangible issue you can help with (whether or not you "caused" the problem to begin with), and so you solve it, without letting your "defensiveness" at being "wrongly accused" get in the way. Or perhaps the other person needs to be "right" because the "customer is always right." In this case, if they are rigidly attached to needing to play a certain role, the identity of "the right customer," why get caught up in that particular drama just because they are? Let go of your own righteousness, and let them be "right." Perhaps they will learn they don't need to become angry to get what they want (or perhaps not), but you have acted with compassion and your own peace of mind has not suffered. You can feel a sense of positive confidence that you acted authentically and with kindness. This type of "softness" is authentic kindness and not soppy, artificial, moralistic kindness; it's the release of judgment. As our rigid sense of self softens and we open up to new possibilities of being, we become empathetic and interconnected with other people. In fact, research is beginning to validate that empathy is typically found in people who register higher levels of satisfaction and happiness in their lives. And higher levels of satisfaction and happiness mean a higher level of mental well-being and health.

EXERCISE:
GETTING TO KNOW YOUR SELVES

This is a contemplation to be performed before you retire for the night. After settling your mind, reflect back to when you first got up that morning. Capture what your first sense of "I" was for the day. For example, "I'm excited about having the day off to go to the beach," or "Sh@#! I've got to rush to make it to that stupid meeting," or "Man, I'm tired." After you capture each experience of who you were, make a simple "I" statement and attach your name. For example, "I was excited John," or "I was agitated John," or "I was tired John." See how your identity and your experience were inextricably connected. Then go through your day and capture multiple experiences using the same formula. You should have a number of labels, like "husband John," "director John," "angry driver John" "hungry John," "father John," and so on. At the end of this exercise, you should be feeling more familiar with how, in fact, we have multiple, even innumerable, identities, even though we experience ourselves as just a single personality. When you conclude, consider: Has your sense of self softened with respect to some of your more rigid, ingrained identities?

CHAPTER EIGHT

Family Game Night: Trivial Pursuits

We have discussed the nature of our misleading mind, and we have presented the simple yet effective mind-training techniques that teach us how to avoid being "misled" by it. Now we just need to put those techniques and understandings into practice. Sounds easy, right?

It can be. But we have to put our task into perspective. For instance, I have noticed that people respond differently to their shortcomings in competitive sports. I see this most commonly in golf. Everyone gets upset with their golf game at some point. But the degree to which someone gets upset seems to have little bearing upon how good of a player they are. What I have noticed is that those players who expect a very high level of performance from their skill set are the ones who get the most upset. The more, and higher level, of expectation they have, the more they will become upset. It is exactly the same with applying mind-training techniques. We should be kind to ourselves and be satisfied with "baby steps."

Surprisingly, our biggest challenges in mind training often involve the smallest events: those everyday distractions that crop up like a stone in your sandal you can't shake out. We gird ourselves to cope with life's biggest, most serious shocks; meanwhile we stumble over cracks in the sidewalk, cursing our stubbed toes and skinned knees. This chapter, then, focuses on those smaller, more common distractions and how to apply these mind-training techniques in the course of an average day. This is, after all, how athletes train their bodies: they warm themselves up and practice gently at first, building strength and stamina over time and, as they are ready, working their way up to bigger and bigger challenges.

Generally speaking, a distraction isn't something that happens "out there." An event becomes a "distraction" only when we are not in control of our impulses, our thoughts, and our emotions. When we gain control over our minds and the disturbing emotions that inevitably arise, we are then able to withstand all kinds of situations, all the stuff life constantly throws at us. We can navigate problems and challenges with greater ease and without disruption to our mental well-being. It takes practice and training to become skilled in this way, and until we are more skilled, our minds can seem fragile and untamed. But also, everyone's personality and temperaments are different. Some situations make us more irritable than others. Already, we can exercise more control and restraint over our harmful emotions in certain circumstances, and less so in others. And sometimes we're better at it than other times. Everyone in the neighborhood can hear an incessantly yapping dog, yet not everyone is driven into a mindless rage because of it. That the person who always seems least disturbed is the dog's owner is a topic for another book.

So, from this moment on, pay attention to your own strengths and weaknesses. Remain aware, without judgment. Don't expect to be equally skilled in all areas right away, or perhaps ever. And as you identify your weaker areas, know that those are places you need to bring more focus. It is amazing how, when we feel particularly interested and engaged in something, nothing seems able to shake our concentration, nothing can dent our good mood. With training, we can remain focused for increasing periods of time and learn to regain our focus at will. Consider your workday right now: When you really need to get a lot of work done, what do you do? Do you need to shut your office door, cancel meetings, turn off the phone, close your email and Internet browser, and set a timer? Do you need to schedule an "at home" day, so you avoid the office entirely? Do you need to make a conscious commitment to stay focused and engaged until the task is finished? Then do you clench your teeth and grind out what needs to be done, feeling stressed the entire time?

In fact, distraction in the workplace is one of the leading factors of low productivity. There is even a new field of study called Interruption Science. We think we're working hard on something, but in reality we skip back and forth among activities all the time. Look at the way we use our computer, for example. It has been well documented that, once we leave the window we are working in, we spend an average of twenty seconds on any one computer window before switching. We go back to our original task 40 percent of the time. The other 60 percent we wander off to another distraction. We have a few emails open, as well as our Internet browser. We hear that "ding" saying that a new email has come in, switch windows to see what the new email is, then quickly check our Facebook page, notice someone has posted a YouTube video of a double rainbow in Yosemite, and, while on YouTube, quickly check out the most popular videos for the day. By this time, ten minutes have passed, and what were we doing again? Then a few minutes later our cell phone vibrates, and on and on it goes.

Our modern culture is designed to be distracting. It's the basic principle of capitalism and advertising, and it could be seen as the general "philosophy" of modern life: pleasure and enjoyment are most important, and nothing is more pleasurable than what is new, better, more. If having our desires met created lasting satisfaction, we wouldn't need to seek any newer or better ways to feel pleasure, and American commerce would screech to a halt. Yet, as we've seen, desire only perpetuates itself, and if we ever do find ourselves sated, advertisers stand ready to create new desires, and we stand ready to accommodate them. Black-and-white television truly made us happy once, but not anymore. We need high-definition, flat-screen, plasma color TVs, with not just the four major network channels or the dozens of standard cable channels, but the hundreds of specialty and niche channels now available, along with movies on demand and direct access to the Internet and... where does it ever stop?

And, honestly, is anyone happier now than they were ten, twenty, fifty years ago because they have more pleasures and, thus, more distractions? I think not. Thus, it is clear to me that our pleasure philosophy is flawed. What we really need is to get control of our mind and learn to focus from the inside out. And we need to do this within the context of the lives we already lead. The other approach — trying to control and fend off the onslaught of products and messages designed to "make us happy"; in other words, trying to effect inner change by changing the world — seems literally impossible.

THE FOUR TRIVIAL PURSUITS

As the Tibetan text the Lam Rim reveals, Buddhism teaches that people spend their lives pursuing eight "Trivial Pursuits." Since these pursuits are, in essence, paired opposites, I've condensed them into an easier-to-remember list of the *Four Trivial Pursuits*:

1. We *seek abundance* and *avoid scarcity*.
2. We *seek fleeting pleasures* and *avoid discomfort*.
3. We *seek praise and compliments* and *shun criticism and blame*.
4. We *pursue a good reputation and prominence* and *shy away from disgrace and dishonor*.

The Four Trivial Pursuits are another way to categorize the disturbing emotions, as well as the aspects of the misleading mind. They provide a useful framework for recognizing the nature of particular distractions in our lives. Or, seen in a positive light, these are the "problems" that form the essential tools of mind training. Let's look at these areas, and as we do, evaluate for yourself to what degree they play a significant role in interrupting your mental health.

1. Seeking Abundance, Avoiding Scarcity

With the First Trivial Pursuit — *seeking abundance and avoiding scarcity* — I have taken the liberty of expanding upon the traditional phrasing of seeking "wealth" and avoiding "poverty." Some people will tell me that they understand the trap of materialism, and they want no part of it. They say they are content with their level of material well-being. I believe them and appreciate their values. But, I am still suspicious. People can have altruistic intentions, but it is difficult to completely let go of the desire for more, nor is it easy to not fear losing what one has. This is the way in which "money corrupts." When one suddenly falls into an inheritance, or gets a big job bonus or wage increase, this newfound abundance can very quickly and easily become a distraction. Isn't it wonderful, all the possibilities and things that more wealth provides? And what does it hurt to buy lottery tickets now and then, on the off chance you'll luck into abundance? It is also interesting to me how much suffering arises when one's financial status becomes threatened. During the recent recession, most people have had to "cut back." This is both painful and the source of increasing anxiety. We get used to a certain level of lifestyle and comfort, and losing it, even though we may have previously lived quite happily for years on less-extravagant means, is quite discomforting.

This is why I prefer to expand upon this distraction. The primary aim of this distraction is to "get more." This mentality alone is a huge distraction in many people's lives and, we could say, is the goal of most business enterprises. Additionally, it is important to expand our investigation of this distraction to include the numerous side effects of this mentality. Pursuing abundance, and avoiding scarcity, does not have to be about the amount of actual money in your bank account, nor is it related to any cultural, social, or economic definition of "wealth" or "poverty." Instead, it is a mindset that raises many *emotional* issues. These emotional issues are universal and affect everyone, regardless of income, class, or lifestyle. As we all know, how we relate emotionally to abundance and scarcity often bears no relation to our resources or how much money we have. While it's a bit of stereotype, it's also true: There are rich people who live like frightened paupers because they are consumed with anxiety over protecting their immense wealth, and there are poor people who live with the emotional ease of kings because they rarely let concern for income and lifestyle distract them.

In our everyday lives, just about everyone desires to raise their income. In the United States, this is a central aspect of the "American Dream." We aspire to achieve a more comfortable existence than the one we were born into, and there is certainly nothing wrong with pursuing a better life, particularly for those who live in truly impoverished circumstances. As a society, we should endeavor to build a world in which everyone has "enough" to live a healthy existence. Yet it is important to be honest with ourselves. Do we ever really feel we have *enough?* Can you say honestly right now that you have "enough," that what you possess is adequate and sufficient? There is no objective standard for "enough." It is purely an emotional judgment, a label, an evaluation of our own condition, and a function of our desires and personal values. As such, we have to be vigilant. It is extremely easy to get caught up in emotional distractions related to our desires for abundance and fears of scarcity. So when we notice disturbing emotions of anxiety, fear, envy, greed, and more arising when we think about wealth, we must practice looking squarely at both the emotion and the subject, the one experiencing the disturbing emotion, and investigate how they exist merely through the misleading mind's creation of them. The misleading mind, remember, sees the wealth to be achieved as really existing, truly. The misleading mind also is adhering to a belief system that is saying, "More will make you happier." We forget that this very wealth is like an illusion. There are some renowned street artists who create sidewalk art that looks like real gold. For a few minutes people are fooled by what looks like gold nuggets on the sidewalk, and they will actually bend down to pick them up only to realize they are just clever three-dimensional drawings. The perception and the emotions accompanying the pursuit of wealth, and all of our distractions, are similar to reaching for illusory coins on the sidewalk...except we keep doing it over and over again. By applying these and other methods we are able to let these feelings go and regard what we have in the present moment as "enough."

Western and US society are no help here. We are bombarded with the "lifestyles of the rich and famous," and while we may not choose to pursue *the highest* levels of wealth, we are encouraged to aspire for more than we have. Thus, becoming rich is a primary motivator for a large number of people in the modern world. Young people are taught that the primary purpose of getting a good education and a good career is to become wealthy, to "get ahead." This cultural value is conveyed and indoctrinated into us at a very young age through every medium: music, television, film, and more. The lesson we learn is that "enough" is never enough. Instead, we are encouraged to aspire to excess, to accumulate more than we need, that "greed is good," since that is where real, lasting pleasure lies. We may laugh when we hear that Imelda Marcos, wife of the former president of the Philippines, had over two thousand pairs of shoes. Of course, that's a ridiculous way to spend one's money. It's excessive to the point of waste. But, then, how different was Imelda Marcos from the rest of us? She had enough money to do anything she wanted, without limit, and so she did. Perhaps we condemn her shoe fetish, since it's so clearly self-centered, but few fault her for being wealthy. We'd all like that particular "problem," right?

In addition, one fundamental purpose of nearly every business is to create wealth. No matter what product or service a business produces, no matter how altruistic its founding goals, it also must generate a profit to *stay* in business. Of course, some businesses are created solely to generate wealth, but all must focus on creating a profit to some degree, and it is very easy for the focus on profit to overwhelm all other agendas. We get excited when a new contract is generated; the monthly profit/loss statement can become the most important standard for how the company is doing; company decisions can turn on how they will affect the stock performance and ensure profits and wealth for shareholders. Thus, for many, it's in the nature of their jobs to be concerned about wealth creation every single moment of the workday. We aren't likely to hear our company's president say, "Okay, we're good enough. We're not going to seek to 'achieve' more success. In fact, we're going to share our abundance with our competitors." We might wish society and business were different — that, say, they adhered more strongly and strictly to a set of higher, more altruistic values like generosity, sharing, caring, and concern for the larger community's welfare. Perhaps, in your chosen profession or particular job, that's true. Nevertheless, the real issue is not the profit focus of business, nor the rightness or wrongness of corporate values in Western culture — it is our individual attitude, our personal values, and our mental capacity to cope with disturbing emotions and not be "distracted" by them. We can still do our jobs, and do them well, while cultivating wholesome, positive emotions within ourselves. If we "blame" our job, our company, or the values of US society for our unhealthy attachment to wealth, we are the ones who suffer. If we do this, we are merely justifying our disturbing emotions of greed and envy. Yet it becomes a win-win if we accompany our positive mindset with an accumulation of success and resources. Admittedly, we have a big challenge to not be distracted by the lure, the buzz, and the high that profit and wealth bring. But if we would foster our own mental health, we must do this, and there's no better place than within the daily grind of our jobs. We spend most of our lives at work, which means we have endless opportunities to practice overcoming this particular distraction.

The reverse of "greed" is the "poverty mentality." This is when we are overwhelmed with fears of poverty, and our actions are driven by avoidance of "losing" what we have. This "poverty consciousness" can exist in anyone, regardless of their means or income level. It is marked by a stingy, miserly, or nongenerous attitude, or perhaps by a fearful anxiety about not having enough and a hypervigilance about spending or sharing and even guarding and hoarding what we do have. Thus, in one's mind, we live in a realm of scarcity to such a degree that we never seem to be able to relax and enjoy what we have or to practice generosity with others. Again, I want to emphasize that I'm discussing the disturbing emotion of fear as it relates to scarcity, not to actual poverty; striving to obtain adequate food, medical care, and housing for oneself and one's family, in this context, is not a "distraction." But a poverty mindset, in which what we have is never enough, certainly is, for it increases our suffering while being wholly unrelated to our actual physical or life circumstances. Perhaps Howard Hughes is the most famous example of what this means. He was unbelievably wealthy, yet he lived like a vagrant. From all appearances, he lived a very tortured life that no amount of actual wealth could cure. Thus, to heal the "poverty mentality," you don't need more money, you need a different mindset.

I have a friend whose mother lives in Europe. Her mother has been run out of town for owing money to everyone. She owns a house that is too big for her, and yet she will not sell it. She always feels like she is on the verge of homelessness and will scam and cajole loans and favors from both people she knows and those she does not. She has exploited her children because she is worried she will not have enough money, but all of her needs are met through various forms of rental income. Looking in from the outside, things really are not that bad for her, but in any case, she constantly exhibits the self-pitying, "poor me" attitude that can also be a signal of this poverty mentality.

For the best education in how abundance and scarcity are states of mind, visit one of the world's poorer countries. For years I lived in Nepal, by any measure an impoverished nation, and yet I found that the majority of the people I met felt relatively content. They were not blind to the wealth available in other places, but they remained content with their own lives. Of course, not all were content. There were those you met who would complain about how poor they were, even though they had sufficient means equal to their fellow citizens. These particular people *felt* "poor," and invariably, their main focus when meeting you was to see what they could get from you. The Nepalese have a saying for these kinds of people: "When these beggars meet a man, all they see are his pockets." That is the poverty mentality. So, pay attention when you meet someone or go out to lunch with friends: Are you looking for what they can give you? Do you complain about how hard times are for you? Or are you content with your situation and happy to share what you have?

2. Seeking Fleeting Pleasures, Avoiding Discomfort

The Second Trivial Pursuit is when we *seek fleeting pleasures and avoid discomfort*. We've already discussed this issue throughout the book, so I won't repeat it at length here. In essence, these distractions are rooted in our confusion between ephemeral sensual pleasures and lasting emotional happiness and contentment. Pleasure is not in itself a bad thing, just like wealth in itself is not good or bad, but neutral. Our attitudes toward them are what we must pay attention to, and when we recognize any of the disturbing emotions, we should regard them as red flags warning that we need to practice mind training and shift our focus. We seek pleasure, obviously, because it feels good, and if we don't become attached to or dependent on momentary pleasant feelings or confuse them with the actual achievement of happiness, then we might say there is no "problem."

But seeking fleeting pleasures can be a zero-sum game, and even leave us feeling worse afterward. What are your "personal pleasures," and how do you go about satisfying them? Become familiar with yourself and your habits, and pay attention to the ways you seek happiness. One way to judge how "attached" we are is to evaluate how we feel when we are denied the pleasure. Do you become agitated? Grumpy? Manic at trying to figure out some alternative way of fulfilling the pleasure? We need to reconsider what it is we think we're trying to accomplish. Then, ask yourself, "Do I want to be in control of pleasure, and thus my life, or do I want the mindless pursuit of pleasure to control me?" In this way, assuming you wish to be in control of your life, you stake a claim upon your real happiness. At this point, standing up to the attempts of the desire for pleasure to control you, seeing this pursuit not as a path to happiness but a path to discontent, the whole emotional dynamic, as if embarrassed at being exposed, will dissipate and dissolve into the sky of your mind like a cloud.

There are other signs of distraction to watch for. Like the marathon runner we read about earlier, perhaps we find that we keep needing "more" to get that good feeling, and the normal distraction of pleasure now becomes exaggerated: we continually need a bigger TV, a faster car, a superior resort hotel, more muscles, better sex, more sports channels, and so on. Also, we may find that we pursue some or all of our pleasures as a means to "escape" feelings of anxiety, depression, anger, and so on. Then you know you're also practicing avoidance in a way that will not only never bring lasting relief but oftentimes increases the problem you are trying to avoid.

This pleasure-principle dynamic operates twenty-four hours a day, seven days a week, to the point where most of our day might be focused on avoiding discomforts through fleeting pleasures. It should be understood that the problem begins in the very next instant after we experience or perceive something. In all perceptions there is either a pleasant, unpleasant, or neutral feeling. When we see a person walking by, after the initial recognition of their blond hair, blue jeans, and tan skin, we have a sensation that is registered in our mind as either pleasant or pleasurable, unpleasant or uncomfortable, or neutral. Then grasping follows: we want more of the pleasurable sensation (to have another cappuccino), less of the unpleasant sensation (to speed away from an intersection after waiting interminably at a lengthy red light), or just mindlessly maintaining the neutral feeling (to "veg out" as we walk through the parking lot to the grocery store). Whatever we are doing gets evaluated in this way. When things are not as pleasurable as expected, we become disappointed, sad, agitated. If they are pleasurable, we begin to cling: "If only I could afford another half-hour massage." "Let me call work and see if we can extend our vacation for another few days." This isn't to say that getting a massage or going on a beach vacation is wrong or bad. But we must see them for what they are and nothing more; if we don't, the very pleasures we enjoy will turn to disappointment and become impediments to our happiness.

Indeed, try this: Rather than setting yourself up for frustration and dissatisfaction, seek inner contentment through mind training *before* going on vacation, getting a massage, or seeing a movie, and see how that *improves* your experience of these "pleasures." One way you can make a significant impact is just to predict what your mind might do once you're in the pleasurable experience and then to consciously be aware of how you would normally get caught. This "spotlight" on one's habitual patterns, by anticipating pleasure's strategies, is a powerfully disarming intervention for your future discontent. It really works.

3. Seeking Praise, Shunning Blame

The Third Trivial Pursuit is *seeking praise and compliments and shunning criticism and blame*. This set of distractions illuminates how attached we are to our ego's version of our "self," as well as to how attached we are to the perceptions of mind. That is, when we look for praise or shun being criticized, we are simply umpires calling our personal balls and strikes, but these judgments are concepts that exist only in our mind. Neither the "self" that judges nor the judgments themselves have any inherent reality since they are merely mental labels ascribed to some kind of event either inside or outside of us. But do we react to them this way in our everyday lives?

I always cringe when I hear someone say something to the effect of: "Can I just offer you some constructive criticism?" I cringe because I've noticed that people really cannot take criticism very well — constructive or otherwise. True, some people are better than others at receiving criticism, or even blame, but I have found that even the toughest recipients can only take a few comments before they shut down or become defensive. Why is that? Simply said, as we discussed in chapter 7, it is because we have fused our sense of self with the "role" or identity that is being criticized, and we forget that all judgments are mental concepts that are limited and malleable (per chapter 3) and frequently the product of the other person's mistaken fusion with their self-created identity.

Naturally, at work, in school, with sports, we thrive on compliments and "attaboys." There is much research that demonstrates that workers perform better when they are praised, encouraged, and given positive feedback on what they are doing right. In and of itself, that is not really a problem. The problem arises when, as in all of our issues, we adhere or cling to praise — when we shape our efforts and our "self" primarily in response to praise and compliments. Then, as a result, we will seek to earn the reward of praise and feel we need it in order to be happy or perform well.

I have a confession to make: When I was a student entering high school, around the ninth grade, I began to slip in my school performance. Something changed in the way I was being taught and the transition from junior high school (or middle school) to high school was a bit radical. No matter how hard I tried, I just couldn't get the system down. I had been an above-average student, but now I really didn't know what was going on, especially in the more academic classes like science, math, and so on. No matter what I did, I got crummy grades. I wasn't failing, but I was barely hanging on. Finally, because nothing I tried was really working, I slowly began cheating on my assignments and tests. I would take cheat sheets into tests in the form of small pieces of paper that I'd hide under my legs on my chair, or I'd write notes on my arm and wear a long-sleeve shirt the day of the test. The funny thing is that I didn't really get great grades even when I cheated, but I was at least feeling more confident that I wouldn't bomb the exam. If the Internet had been around in those days, I'm sure my written homework assignments and reports would have been better. All I could do was copy whole passages out of the *World Book Encyclopedia*. Why did I do all of this? To avoid my mother's criticism. She used to examine our report cards and then put us down for any minor flaw. In other words, I preferred (unseen) cheating to the public disgrace I felt and the type of person my mother's criticism and judgment made me out to be. Even if it was based on falsehoods, I wanted the reputation of a "self" that did well in school.

How dependent are you on being praised for your work? When you offer companionship, warmth, and love to your friends and to your partner, do you need it acknowledged? Are you less friendly and affectionate if someone fails to notice your attentiveness and seemingly takes you for granted? Does someone's criticism immediately make you defensive and even lash right back with your own criticism? How much of what you do is motivated or driven by the need to be valued and recognized by other people? How important is it to hear positive words and not hang around with "negative" people? Clearly, no one wants to be around people who are deliberately mean, who invariably disrupt a peaceful, wholesome environment. The real question is: How "personally" do you take any negative or positive comment? What makes these issues "distractions" is our own internal reactions and perspective. That's what we can change, and where we will find contentment, despite the slings and arrows others may throw our way.

As you go about your day, observe your own anticipation of and reactions to judgment, real or imagined. What particular "self" demands extra praise? Are we put out if we make a meal for our kids and they don't seem to care or comment at all, but we don't have the same reaction if we cook for our spouse or for friends? If so, then perhaps our "parent" self is in need of extra support. How about when you do chores around the house, especially when you do a task no one asked or expected you to do? Do you feel a little hurt or unrecognized if no one comments on your efforts? What happens if they notice, but then they say something like, "Oh! Thanks for hanging the pictures, but don't you think they're a little too low?" If a cloud of resentment blows through, notice it and analyze (as a kind of broad awareness) how the person's comment is neither good nor bad until, like the umpires, you call their comment a ball or strike in your mind. Their comments "ain't nothin' till you call them."

Indeed, it seems like there is no area in life where our judgments don't insert themselves. We are constantly evaluating ourselves and others. I don't know a single person who benefits from the backseat driver, and yet the backseat driver exists in just about every group and culture that drives. Someone always knows better and is eager to share their thoughts even if they are counterproductive to the task at hand!

What's also fascinating is how often envy or jealousy of someone else's success or achievement gets cloaked in criticism. We may hear ourselves or someone else say, "It's amazing to me that Brian is such a successful orthodontist when he's such an unfriendly guy." Or, "She's quite attractive for a woman with two face lifts, isn't she?" When we hear ourselves say things like this, can we recognize how, perhaps, the self is being threatened by another's success? And which self is being threatened, anyway? A very common workplace situation, one that provides material for many a TV sitcom, is the urge to criticize the people in charge. But when we do, are we fairly commenting upon the work of another, or merely voicing justification for our own performance and seeking recognition for qualities we may not feel so sure we possess? I once consulted for a nonprofit that cultivated an underground value: criticizing the job of the director. By this I mean that the cause of all the problems within the organization was overly projected upon the director. This had gone on over a long time and several different directors. It seemed that whenever there was a problem, rather than each worker assessing if they had some degree of accountability, the director was always blamed for the difficulty. As a result, a cultural laziness, or a lack of accountability, persisted within and hampered the organization.

When you teach a class for the first time, show someone a piece of writing, or present your just-purchased new car, how much does it matter to you that you hear encouragement, praise, and compliments? How much do you fish for those comments? "Pretty sweet car, eh?" we might proudly say to our friends. Can we see that we're not talking about the car (or the writing, or the success of the lesson), but looking to bolster our own sense of self? It is important to look at when and how much we seek compliments and shun criticism. When we investigate in this way, become familiar with ourselves, then we can put our happiness back in our own hands by making a stand against a mind that is at the mercy of what other people say and think about us.

4. Pursuing a Good Reputation, Shying Away from Dishonor

The Fourth Trivial Pursuit is to *pursue a good reputation and prominence and shy away from disgrace and dishonor*. This is similar to seeking praise and shunning blame, but seems more directly linked with our sense of self and how it "shows up" to others. This distraction can be more aligned with our ideas of "who we are" and the social judgment of us as a person, rather than merely the verbal judgments that accompany particular actions.

In fact, like the other Trivial Pursuits, there is nothing inherently wrong with valuing the good opinion of others and maintaining a positive self-image. In a way, this is a useful, productive thing to have. Typically, when members of a group respect one another, the group is more effective and able to accomplish its goals. Nearly every endeavor in life is dependent upon the cooperation and assistance of other people — this pertains to just about every task facing us. Thus, what concerns us here is the overly focused attitude that seeks to continually enhance one's self-image, or one's business, in the eyes of others. To what degree is enhancing and protecting our self-image a major object of our life's endeavors? We read about journalists who write articles that are false just so they can be seen by their peers as great reporters. Scientists will fake the results of their experiments both to protect themselves from losing status and to rise to a higher level of recognition within the scientific community. And, on the reverse side of the coin, a politician may resort to illegal activity in order to prevent a "dirty little secret" from reaching the public domain. Lying about your golf score is a way to maintain your reputation as a certain caliber of golfer. Even being less than honest with your spouse when she asks, "Unlike your buddy Rick, at least *you* never look at other women, do you?" can be an effort to protect your reputation, your self-image, in her eyes. In addition, as we seek to create a meaningful life, do we let the pursuit of a good name, notoriety, and recognition become a self-defeating end in itself?

Our struggles here reveal how much we cling to our own self-image and its outer representation as our "social image." It is important to have a healthy self-image and be accepted within our community, to have a sense of self-worth and an appreciation for our accomplishments. However, a healthy self-image is the by-product of a healthy approach to life. When we are convinced that our self-image is something concrete and real, and we make it the actual end goal we are seeking, it proves not only elusive and unsustainable but a big waste of our precious life. The reason is because we are putting value and effort into developing something that is changeable and ephemeral, so it can never offer any real contentment. The energy needed to build our reputation, maintain it, and then regenerate it once it has waned is both stressful and anxiety-provoking; certainly the opinions of others are outside of our control and, at times, easily swayed by their own disturbing emotions. And, finally, whoever we want to be recognized for is not really who we are anyway. As we discussed in chapter 7, any self-image we build for ourselves is, actually, false; any identity we have is based on a context that can and will change, and thus neither is truly lasting. So we should appreciate a nice reputation when we have one, while knowing that it most likely will not last or extend into other areas of our life. If we base our self-image and self-worth on earning a few letters after our name, like "PhD" or "CEO," this will not make us a "Great Parent" or a "Dependable Friend." Conversely, we can be a "Great Mom" at home and a "Dumb Cop" or an "Ineffectual Teacher" at work, and so on. Then, our school may change principals, and our reputation at work might change into "The Type of Progressive Teacher We're Looking For." The trap is when we put all our efforts into sustaining and "freezing" particular self-images. Then, once the image fades or changes, or is threatened or questioned, we have to go into damage control and build it back up. Then, in practice, we end up defending our image, our reputation, a process that very often distracts us from effectively dealing with the issues that need solving. It's like this:

- "If you're such a great therapist, why aren't I getting any better?" (Rather than defend yourself, perhaps this client needs a different type of therapy or a "better fit" therapist.)
- "A top-level CEO doesn't deliver crappy earnings like these." (Perhaps the recession is to "blame," or perhaps there are management or production issues that need fixing.)
- "If you're such a good mother, why does your child cry constantly while you're at the supermarket?" (Perhaps you're a fine mother, but your child has a medical issue.)
- "With grades like these, you'll never get into college. Hope you like digging ditches and bagging groceries." (Perhaps your parents want you to be a different person, and college really isn't for you, or your talents lie in other fields, like the arts.)
- "Your research is pretty sloppy and doesn't support your findings. Have you thought about giving up your own research and working for a company?" (Perhaps this contains some truth: your affinity is for another branch of science, but you've been trying to follow in your father's footsteps.)

Sometimes we pursue identities because we feel we are "supposed to," and when we aren't successful, it's a sign that it's not something we really desire or is a good fit for our personality. We'd do better to let go of our attachment to a certain identity (like "field scientist"). But at any time, if we take criticisms or problems personally, as if they define who we are, then we miss the real issue and solution. Then, by our mistaken focus on our own reputation, we make problems worse and simply do more damage to our standing in the eyes of others. These kinds of threats to our self-image, our credibility, happen every day, so what do we do about them? When you feel the sting of a challenge to your reputation, your self-image, your "good name," do you become defensive, deflecting or dismissing the comments of the other person? When this happens, can you stop yourself, reflect on what the other person is saying without reacting, and then act upon those comments you find to be true (and move on from the comments that have no use)? To openly investigate in this way immediately changes the dynamic of protecting your sense of self and allows you to attend to the issues at hand with a more balance, centered mindset.

To want to improve ourself and increase our qualifications and expertise is not the concern as long as we are not controlled by worrying about what others think. It is often our concern about our reputation that will freeze us from offering our ideas at meetings or asking questions in class. It is our concern for our reputation that might give us the jitters when applying for a new position. We should not be overly worried about how our mistakes will look to others; everyone makes mistakes, or stumbles, or has skills they need to develop, and so our focus should be on improving ourselves for our own well-being as well as the well-being of others. When we consider the well-being of others in conjunction with our own well-being, we will be protected from being led down the road of antisocial or destructive behavior — which the concept of "not being concerned about our reputation" may seem to allow. It could be deduced that if we are not concerned with our reputation or self-image, we can do whatever we want. This is a gross misunderstanding of this trivial pursuit. The reason we seek not to be obsessed with our reputation is so we can be of more benefit to ourselves and others. So when standing up to the destructive hooks of reputation, we also must assess our actions to make sure they aren't destructive in other ways. Someone who acts antisocially, for example, may seem not to care about his reputation, but at the same time he is not concerned about his own well-being and, particularly, the well-being of others. Willfully undermining or damaging one's reputation is not the approach to take either. The practice is, to be clear, a mental endeavor that is designed to allow you not to be owned by the practices of reputation building. It is not a good reputation that is the problem — it is the obsession with having a good reputation (or avoiding disgrace). Be alert to signs that your main concern is with your reputation, and recognize that this is only bolstering your false sense of self and affecting your equilibrium and inner balance. Slowly shift from an outer-directed focus on reputation to an inner-directed focus on ego-less problem solving, positive impact, and effectiveness. This shift in focus is how mind training helps us to creating a meaningful life of lasting happiness.

I remember in the early 1980s, while living in Nepal, I had an exchange with my spiritual mentor, Lama Thubten Yeshe. I was helping him answer some of his correspondence, and there was a letter from his home monastery, called Sera-je. Sera-je was originally based in Lhasa, Tibet, and housed over five thousand monks. After the 1959 Chinese invasion of Tibet, thousands of Tibetans sought refuge in India, where they reestablished Sera-je in southern India with just a fraction of the original number of monks. In Tibet, Sera-je monastery had been famous for being one of the major monastic universities. These huge monasteries had, and continue to maintain, a rigorous educational system. A monk who was inclined could strive to attain a highly respected degree as a Geshe — a degree that might be equivalent to a PhD in philosophy, psychology, and metaphysics all wrapped into one. The Geshe degree, traditionally speaking, took at least twenty-five years of study and was awarded to only eighteen monks per year. Candidates would often have to wait years for their opportunity to take the three-day public oral exam, which would be witnessed by thousands of onlookers during the Tibetan New Year. In the early 1960s, as Tibetans fled from Chinese-occupied Tibet, the Geshe exam process was disrupted, and it particularly affected those monks who had completed their studies and were waiting for an exam date. Lama Thubten Yeshe fell into this category. In the late seventies and early eighties many monks were "grandfathered" into the Geshe degree; they were given a kind of amnesty for their exam requirements. There was to be a special ceremony, I believe with an abbreviated exam, for these monks who had dispersed to India and Nepal and other countries. The letter to Lama Yeshe that I read was his invitation to this ceremony, and I thought, "Finally, Lama will get the recognition he deserves." I asked him, rather excitedly, "Oh, so you're going to go to India to receive your degree?" To which he replied, "Why do I need another name like 'Geshe'? I already have two good names, 'Thubten' and 'Yeshe.'" When speaking of himself, he did not even use the honorific term "Lama" by which others addressed him. I was struck by Lama Yeshe's total renunciation of notoriety. This is what it means to move beyond the distractions of the Trivial Pursuits.

KEEP INSPIRATION FROM BECOMING DISTRACTION

As humans, we have access to a deeper spiritual and creative reality. Most people have had a spiritual experience in their lives — an epiphany, a moment of revelation or insight, an "aha" moment that most likely occurred when they did not expect it. Such an experience can happen when spending intimate time with a loved one or in a deep conversation with someone we respect. It can also happen when communing with nature or anytime when we are out of our usual routine and our minds and spirits are open. Or, we may be seeking insights directly — in a therapy session, a seminar, a meditation retreat, a sweat lodge, or a vision quest. These insights can even occur during intensely emotional events and passages, like childbirth, grieving someone's death, coping with an illness, and so on. Through such experiences, we encounter a quality to our human life, our human "being-ness," that is regularly obscured and hidden. This is, in essence, a brief opening of our wisdom eye, allowing us an encounter with our vast, even unlimited human potential. This insight into wisdom reveals the interconnection between beings, the profundity and mystery of life, and the truth of the phrase "there's more to life than what appears to the eye." These are peeks beyond the window of our individuality into the universal nature of consciousness and life.

Of course, like all experiences, these moments of spiritual connection usually do not endure. That is simply the nature of this life, as the Buddha recognized so long ago; everything changes, nothing lasts. What's even more frustrating, however, is how hard it can be to re-create these peak experiences of connection. Why is that? Simply put, it is due to our mental imprints, which produce our habitual tendencies, or conditioning, to see things otherwise, to be distracted. In a way, it is a kind of laziness, particularly when we know better but don't put what we know into practice.

Laxity or *dullness* is easy to understand, if hard to justify. While moments of connection can unexpectedly open before us at times, sustaining them and repeating them take focus and effort. This is the path that mind training leads to, and yet in its incessant focus on "problems," mind training can at times feel very difficult, with little to show for it. So, we get bored; in the moment, it can feel easier to let go of our good intentions and instead "space out." What would we rather do when we get a free hour: surf the Internet or practice focusing our mind and grappling with our disturbing emotions? The primary reason we make this choice is, well, lack of practice. Practice leads to discipline. Discipline arises not from some sort of outer dictum or punishment but because we find when we apply discipline we become better. No one desires to get up at 5:30 in the morning and go run three miles. So, why do people do it? It is because they are "disciplined." A runner sees the benefit of running, enjoys the fruit of consistency, dislikes getting out of shape, and so...runs every morning at 5:30. This is the same kind of discipline I'm referring to, and it is the antidote to laziness and a lackadaisical mind and attitude. The old adage that you get what you pay for is most apt in the discussion of discipline. Perhaps, instead of discipline, we could just say "effort."

At the other end of the scale, we get so caught up in our lives that we "forget" to practice. These are distractions of *excitement* or *overstimulation*, and while these are usually pleasurable emotions, we often confuse them with happiness. Then we become confused and disoriented when the excitement passes and here we are, right where we were before, and no closer to the spiritual connection we meant to be pursuing. Our lives are busy, and we have important things to do, rushing to appointments, making phone calls, catching up with friends, making plans, coping with unexpected emergencies — in short, being so stimulated, engaged, and, yes, distracted that we have quite a hard time stopping suddenly and trying to focus.

Thus, we spend much of our time and mental energy pursuing the "feel-good" aspects of the Four Trivial Pursuits — abundance, pleasure, praise, and a good reputation — while avoiding their uncomfortable opposites. Then, if we ever give ourselves a break from the treadmill of distraction, perhaps from mere exhaustion alone, when do we gather the energy and strength to do the hard work to re-create those inspirational moments that seem to be receding further and further in the distance? It is a choice, remember. And we must be kind to ourselves: kind in encouraging ourselves to do the work and even kind to ourselves to allow a rest so we can gather our energy and resources to be steady in our practice. It is better to move at the steady pace of a snail than with the manic haste of a hare. It is a fact that if a person acts with too much intensity or fervor, they will quickly lose interest or stamina. It is a common adage in meditation instruction, for instance, to meditate for a duration that is shorter than you wish. That way you'll want to come back to your cushion to pursue your practice. If we push ourselves too much, our soft meditation cushion will begin to resemble a bed of nails. So we'll transform our lives with patience and kindness and without making one big effort that tries to re-create our lives in one fell swoop. We will only do so by making a thousand small efforts, using the little windows of awareness and time that we make available, until our habits slowly change and our priorities progressively shift.

Releasing our attachments isn't easy, and it takes time. There is a friend of mine who is very attached to food. Of course, I like food also; who doesn't? However, for my friend food is a very big deal and it can dominate his focus. One time we had arranged to drive north together from Los Angeles to Santa Cruz; I was to follow him in my car. Ironically, we were attending a weekend of teachings with the Dalai Lama, and my friend was very anxious that we leave the very moment the final lecture was done, at 11 AM. The night before, we set up the plan, and in a very agitated fashion, he kept repeating his instructions: "We have to leave right when the teaching ends, at 11, you know? Okay, by 11. And make sure you check out before the teaching and put your bag in your car." I wasn't sure why he was so antsy, but I agreed and followed through with everything. Then, by 11:15 we were on the road, and he was really in a hurry. After about two hours of driving, he called me on my cell phone and told me we were stopping for lunch: we would just make it to his favorite Mexican restaurant, which closed at 2 PM. Now I understood: all of our rushing and his anxiety and pushiness, even from the night before, had to do with his wanting to eat at his favorite Mexican restaurant on the road between Los Angeles and Santa Cruz. This kind of planning and thinking about the future is what is referred to in Buddhist psychology as the motivation that precedes any action. Motivation, or intention, is a huge predictor of our mindset that arises during the actual event. As the saying goes, "If you make appointments, you will be disappointed."

As Alan Wallace pointed out in his book *The Attention Revolution*, "Our very perception of reality is tied closely to where we focus our attention." The tragedy of all this self-distraction is that it prevents us from ever going much deeper than the mundane. Our reality becomes impoverished. But if we can focus so acutely upon getting a good Mexican lunch, finishing a work project late into the night, or helping our child succeed in school, can't we then bring this same level of focus and attention and energy to mind training and improving our lives in the long run? If not, we short-change ourselves spiritually and lock ourselves into patterns of unhappiness. We fail to look at our lives and never become fully aware of our behaviors. John Lennon captured it well: "Life is what happens to you while you're busy making other plans."

THE FOUR TRIVIAL PURSUITS EXERCISES

In a quiet moment, sit with your eyes gently closed and focus your attention upon the breath. As in earlier exercises, first settle the mind on the breath. Then begin to watch the mind and thoughts. Pay attention to how frequently you become distracted. You'll notice that you'll be able to observe consciously for only a few seconds until the mind becomes absorbed in a thought, image, or feeling. When that happens, catch yourself and assign a number to the occurrence, as in "first time," "second time," and so on. Notice how distracted your mind actually is. Perform this exercise, no matter what, for a full ten minutes. Repeat it for at least three days, trying it at different periods of the day. After you've done it for three days, continue with the second half, presented below.

Again, focus your attention upon the breath. Now, identify the quality of your mind each time it loses concentration. When you notice a distraction, see if it falls into one of the Four Trivial Pursuits. If it does, and it most likely will, just label it "seeking pleasure," "looking for praise," and so on. Do not elaborate any more than just labeling, and then return to the breath.

As with all of the daily reflections, their intent is that they will show a microcosm of your whole life, the life that includes you working, exercising, socializing, and so on. Take the learning you are attaining in the reflection and then expand it throughout your daily life. Becoming familiar with the Four Trivial Pursuits in your reflection, for example, is the quickest and most effective way of becoming aware of them in all the other arenas of your life.

CHAPTER NINE

Who Left the Milk Out?

In my family, "mistake making" was unacceptable, nonnegotiable. If the milk was left out, the question that would echo throughout the house was invariably, *"Who left the milk out?!"* It was not an inquiring question. It was meant to establish guilt. The subtext was "We need to know who to blame so we can exact the proper penalty of embarrassment and put-downs in order for you to know how far you are from perfection."

If someone left the milk out in your house, how was it handled? The question can sound innocent enough, but the intention behind the question, the person's mindset, can reveal much about a person's, even a household's, views on mistakes, blame, values, and compassion. Remember Carl and Trisha from chapter 1? They came to me on the verge of divorce because, in part, Trisha would inadvertently leave the milk out on the counter overnight. For them, seemingly trivial issues like this were leading to very serious consequences, and this sort of escalation of problems happens all the time. In our household as well, leaving the milk out became an almost comically exaggerated crime — funny, that is, if it wasn't you who did it and had to suffer the emotional consequences.

What's your knee-jerk reaction when you find the milk still sitting on the breakfast table? Do you become angry? Do you launch an investigation into "who did the evil deed"? When you find that person, do you then blame and shame them so they "learn a lesson" and "don't do it again"? Or, do you acknowledge that someone in the house slipped up, but feel no emotional charge about it? If you discover who that person is, do you say, with genuine good humor, "Hey, don't forget to put the milk away next time, okay?" Or, rarest of all, do you simply put the milk away, without saying anything more about it or feeling anything at all?

Everyone makes mistakes, and every mistake is a learning opportunity. Buddhism would say that the very first "lesson" to be learned is in one's reaction to the mistake itself. Do we react out of ignorance or out of informed awareness? If the former, then it will arise from a self-centered or "me first" attitude, and then in all likelihood our "sense of justice" will confuse the real issue, incorrectly place blame, and quite possibly make the problem worse in emotional terms. If the latter, then our reactions will embody a compassionate ethics that values the ultimate welfare of everyone involved and will in all likelihood lessen the long-term emotional drama or guilt felt by anyone.

This final chapter is about how mind training is not only a way to improve our personal sense of contentment and happiness but also a way to improve the lives of everyone around us, for it gives birth to an ethics that approaches problems differently: as avenues for increasing compassion, understanding, and wisdom. If you value being right, being smart, and looking good, then what do you find when you see the milk sitting out? Most likely, someone else who is wrong, acting stupid, and mistake prone. Can you resist pointing this out to them? In fact, even viewing an event as a mistake can be a mistake in itself. By labeling something a mistake, it sets us up to find a "mistake maker," someone to blame. That's the rule about mistakes:

they are someone's fault. However, it does not have to be so — where is the "mistake" if certain actions lead to inner growth and learning, for oneself or someone else? We have to be careful and be more conscious of the choices we make when we label events. Did Lama Atisha "blame" his cook for all his bad behavior and "mistakes"? Did he not, instead, prefer to have the cook around, someone who, metaphorically speaking, would leave the milk out all the time, just so that Atisha could demonstrate putting away his own anger and judgment?

We can choose our habitual pattern of seeing mistakes and looking for someone to blame, or we can choose to see all circumstances as events from which we might learn and grow. So the next time there's milk left out on the breakfast table, think about what is important for you. Think about what it is you wish to create, what the consequences of your reaction might be. What does your reaction say about who you think you are and who other people are? What effect do you want to have in all your relationships, which includes your relationship with yourself? What kind of imprints will these actions leave on your consciousness that will further compel you to act in the future as well as define who you will be? Think hard about this first, then respond. If you want to heal yourself, then you must become a teacher for yourself, and in this way you become an example and a teacher for others. Increase your own wisdom and awareness, and then others will find the space to learn, improve, and feel confident in your presence. Then it will not much matter "who left the milk out." You will have solved the "crime" in your heart first, so there is no need for punishment, only learning.

AN ETHICS OF HEALTH AND WELL-BEING

An early Buddhist text by Shantideva, the renowned Buddhist author and philosopher of ancient India, says:

If you can solve your problem,
Then what is the need of worrying?
If you cannot solve it,
Then what is the use of worrying?

In other words, when we are faced with a problematic circumstance, disturbing emotions such as worry, anxiety, fear, and frustration are never helpful. They do not aid our understanding, nor do they resolve the real issue. So, resisting their invitations and letting them go is how we, as the saying goes, understand and fix those things we can change and accept those things we cannot.

Ethics and even morals are naturally aligned with our mental health. This means that confirming the "right" action to take can arise through an understanding of our own psychology: what is ethical will always be that which intends to support and foster the long-term mental well-being of ourselves and others. Actions based on compassion, kindness, and wisdom take into account everyone's benefit, not merely our own. When we fail to do this, we can often deduce this also by evaluating our state of mind. As our milk story makes clear: When our actions are driven by anger, attachment, or ignorance, our mind and emotions remain disturbed, as will our relationships with others. Of course, a compassionate, ethical action may also make us feel uncomfortable if it is unfamiliar, and others may criticize our choice, so we cannot make a blanket statement that our mental state will invariably, especially in the immediate moment, reflect our intentions. But the mindset and intentions behind an action are paramount, and they are usually revealed by the ultimate effects of the action. To truly be considered ethical, an action must arise from the intention of resisting harm and hopefully improving the welfare of everyone involved. As His Holiness the Dalai Lama frequently advises: It is best to help. But if you cannot help, then at the very least do no harm.

When we shift our focus from the relief of symptoms (our disturbing emotions) to an awareness of the cause (our misleading mind), we generate the real meaning of ethics. The practice of ethics should be logic based and not driven by some kind of higher authority. That is, actions and laws should be considered "ethical" based upon the motivation of the person and whether they are successful at creating healthier, happier people and a healthier, happier, better-functioning society. Every major religion of the world and every civilized culture is founded on an ethical code of conduct. A robust constitution and legal system is, really, nothing more than an attempt at creating the standards of behavior that will produce a just and wholesome society. Granted, the definition of a "just and wholesome society" may be biased and subjective. Nonetheless, by defining what is meant by a "wholesome society," and what is necessary to achieve it, ethics then establishes the standards of accountability that citizens must follow. Breaching those codes is thus "wrong" because it directly undermines the society that citizens have pledged to create.

Buddhist psychology has its own ethical foundation, one articulated by the Buddha in his Four Noble Truths and based on the Buddhist concept of human perception. While there is a physical world, and it affects us continually and constantly, it is not the "cause" of our state of mind. The conditions of the world contribute to, but do not cause, our internal state of being. Indeed, the physical world does not exist separate from our perception of it, and so any experience of pain or suffering is produced, and thus resolved, internally, within our own mind. In fact, as mentioned earlier, while it is disconcerting that it is so slippery and difficult to distinguish the line between our external and internal worlds, it provides us with a clear standard for action. This is where ethics comes into play: *harmful actions produce unhealthy states of mind and helpful actions produce healthy states of mind.* With this as a guide, we can evaluate our actions by our own state of mind and act in the best interests of others.

The disturbing emotions are all considered unhelpful, and thus unhealthy, states of mind; they are the cause of our suffering, so when we act in ways that increase our disturbing emotions, we are only increasing our suffering and not being helpful to others. An ethical response to the true causes of our distress will produce healthy and helpful states of mind within ourselves, like warmth, affection, a caring attitude, empathy, compassion, patience, and wisdom, to name a few. Further, the only way to promote harmony, balance, and serenity in the world is by fostering our own positive emotions and acknowledging the true cause of suffering — our misleading mind and disturbing emotions.

IGNORANCE: THE ROOT CAUSE

In chapter 4, I listed the three primary afflictive or disturbing emotions that are the cause of all suffering: aversion, attachment, and ignorance. These interact with the Three Conditions listed in chapter 1: that physical pain is unavoidable, that life is changeable and ephemeral, and that we are ignorant of the true nature of reality. In both lists, we've discussed the first two items at length, but in truth, ignorance is at the root of every problem we suffer. This is ignorance of the true nature of our misleading mind and of our conception of self or identity. Being unaware of this, we make the emotional mistakes of aversion and attachment in response to the circumstances of life. Conversely, we "fix" or "solve" these emotional disturbances by developing an accurate perception of how things really exist, of the relative nature of one's self and everything else.

This is the simple proposal of mind training, and it constitutes the approach we should take every time we find ourselves with a disturbed mind. We need to ask ourselves:

1. Am I clinging or attached to something that I don't want to let go of? This is not just about possessions, remember.

It applies most especially to a point of view or opinion that you cling to and don't want to give up. Or perhaps it's the meaning you generated about an old experience, particularly one that provides the rationale for who you are and why you act the way you do. These "stories" or narratives are what create our false sense of self, and clinging to them further perpetuates disturbing emotions. We must break free of these stories and their creations of self.

2. Am I avoiding or wanting to get away from something? This can be anything we feel uncomfortable with or just don't like. Aversion is usually associated with anger and fear, but it includes a host of emotions. When our mind is disturbed by these emotions, our actions will be focused on condemning, eliminating, or pushing away whatever it is we don't like. We desire to be free from what makes us uncomfortable, and if we don't recognize this as our own disturbing emotions, then we act out our anger and fear on others. This is ineffectual. We may, by threats and intimidation, solve the apparent "problem" of others leaving the milk out, but we have not only demonstrated to others our lack of control over ourselves but, more importantly, we have not learned how to cope with our disturbing emotions when something inevitably triggers them again.

3. How is ignorance distorting reality? Remember the adage "We see things that are not there and do not see the things that are." The events unfolding before me are not existing the way I think or perceive them to be. I superimpose all kinds of assumptions, qualities, preconceptions, and distortions upon the experience unfolding before my eyes...and before all my senses, including even my thought. This is not referring to the grosser aspects of ignorance like fogginess, apathy, and indecisiveness. These are considered afflictive

emotions or states of mind that arise *as a result* of the deeper, pervasive ignorance referred to here. Instead, any disturbing emotion should call us back to our focused awareness on the misleading mind's creation of the false sense of self and its misperception of the world, and thus shake us into its opposite experience — the correct perception of "what's there," reality. Once this awareness is achieved, and we have put away worry, it is possible to look at a situation or circumstance and determine if, as Shantideva implies, we can change something and fix the problem, or if we must accept a circumstance as beyond our ability to change it.

By asking yourself this series of questions, you begin to expose the dynamics of your own mind, and you clarify your own misperceptions so you can act in helpful, ethical ways. *And remember*: Any solution to any issue must be accompanied by informed awareness, a synonym for "wisdom." Informed awareness is like a powerful flashlight and the disturbing emotions are like cockroaches — they run from the light of wisdom. Wisdom is what can transform blame into compassion and end suffering immediately and completely in the moment.

ENDING THE BLAME GAME

As we've learned, we tend to wrongly assign blame by pinning our problems, particularly our emotional problems, on something or someone else: we blame our "unsympathetic" boss, or we blame our "unfeeling" spouse, or we say we are angry because some stranger scratched our car door and took off without leaving a note. *All* of this is erroneous. Our afflictions, our disturbing emotions and thoughts, arise only when we remain ignorant of who we really are. Our emotions and states of mind are not us — *they are something we possess*. In fact, it might be more accurate to say *we are possessed by them*, by our afflictive emotions. As we've discussed, all thoughts and concepts are objects of the mind. We can possess these thoughts and concepts, but we are by definition *separate* from them, even if we are interdependent. We have them, but we are not them. Thus, when we define ourselves by our afflictions, we do so in ignorance of our true nature, and then they are ruling us and writing our story for us. Our identity becomes attached to our afflictions, so that they seemingly become merged, fused, as if they are one, such as when we say, "I am nervous" or "I am depressed." As Tibetan scholars tell us, it's more correct to say, "I *have* nervousness or depression, but I can't *be* nervousness or depression."

It is for this reason that the most effective, and perhaps the most ethical, approach to any problem is to shift our focus from the outer "circumstance" that sparks our reaction to the inner circumstances of the reaction itself. This is how we honestly take responsibility for ourselves. Accepting the "blame" for our own emotions and their effects upon others is really just being accountable. To look inwardly at the cause of our struggles is not really even to "blame" ourselves. It just acknowledges the correct source of suffering, which is our internal emotions and misperceptions, and it acknowledges that only we ourselves have control over these. In the end, if we must blame something, and we want to do it properly and correctly, then we should blame ignorance and the afflictive emotions that arise because of it. In this way, we can't truly blame ourselves or anyone, for each person shares the same predicament: a misleading mind that causes confusion and mistakes the source of problems.

For instance, we might say, "You hurt me by what you said," but seen in this light, the entire accusation unravels. If the other's intention was to hurt, then they are suffering from their own disturbed emotions and misperceptions; perhaps they mistakenly blame us for their difficulties. Thus their actions reveal their own ignorance and lack of control — which surely calls for compassion and understanding, not punishment. If they didn't intend to hurt us, then any harm they caused was inadvertent, accidental, and at that point, will lashing out in anger or defensiveness benefit either of us? It will probably only make them defensive and resentful: "I never meant to hurt you! How dare you accuse me of being mean." But if we take responsibility for our feelings, hold ourself accountable for them, even take the opportunity to understand what sparked them ("Oh, I guess I got tricked into thinking I'd be happy if my 'good spouse' self got some acknowledgment when I do chores"), then "blaming" becomes irrelevant.

As we've discussed, the reasons disturbing emotions arise are various. Perhaps we are attached to our good reputation, and we need praise and compliments and cannot abide any criticism. Or we may be clinging to a particular identity, as "the life of the party," and we feel threatened if someone else is stealing the attention away. This isn't to say that everything that happens is just "in your mind." If a tornado destroys our home, that is certainly a viable circumstance that very likely will cause many disturbing emotions, such as fear, loss, attachment, and sorrow. It is understandable these emotions might be stimulated. Yet, do we "blame" the tornado? What does that get us? How effective is it in healing our emotions and our pain? In the end, we must turn inward and "make our peace" with this unexpected trauma and move on. For Shantideva, this is acknowledging and accepting what can't be changed.

From a Buddhist psychological point of view, something outside of us cannot be the direct cause of an inner problem. It can be the condition or circumstance we must deal with, but not the cause of our emotions or a state of mind. When we look at the issue of blame, we must make a distinction between a cause and a condition. If our boss is critical of us, the boss and his criticism are a *condition*. Our emotional reactions (actually, the misperceptions they are based on) are the *cause* of our difficulty. Since suffering is mental, its cause must also be of the same nature, mental. Simply put, if one is confused about who or what to blame, follow this "rule": Physical results have physical causes. Mental results have mental causes.

We must be vigilant in putting aside blame. You are not responsible, perhaps, when your car is dented, but you are responsible for your feelings about it. You are 100 percent responsible for your internal experience, and many people rile at this thought. We are so out of touch with our internal world that we believe that outside conditions, which include other people, control our happiness and our mental well-being. And as long as we believe this, it will continue to be true.

This process of "experiencing and reacting" happens constantly, twenty-four hours a day, seven days a week, 365 days a year, for our entire life. Typically, we are not aware of the process as it is happening within us. This is why ignorance is considered a root cause of the afflictive emotions. Ignorance may seem like bliss but, actually, bliss is one of the things we are missing when we remain ignorant. Thus, the true object of blame is stupidity, ignorance, confusion, and bewilderment. Most of the time, we keep ourselves too distracted to see properly what is happening in our life and our world.

Though it is a small example of irritation, the following exchange I had with a client is a good example of how blame and misperception are inextricably linked, and of how, to effectively solve problems, we must focus inward first, rather than on the "other."

On Wednesday morning at 9:15 AM, I received the following email from a client: "10?"

I was perplexed by this single number and question mark. Therefore, I went back through earlier emails to see what she was referring to. I had remembered that our usual Tuesday appointment had been changed at her request because she had a scheduling conflict. This is what she emailed on Monday: "We have an unplanned meeting at work I should be around to make sure things are going well, does wed work?"

I wrote back: "No problem I got my own bowling pins to juggle."

That's when I realized: My client expected me to show up in forty-five minutes for a two-hour meeting that I had, in that moment, no plans to attend. On Monday, when I had told her "no problem," she assumed I meant that meeting on "wed" was no problem. But I hadn't paid attention to "wed"; I just meant it was no problem to reschedule. Now I was agitated, annoyed, and frustrated. I was in the middle of working on another project when her "10?" email arrived, and I had an aversion to making a shift. I didn't want to drop everything to meet with my client. I had planned out my morning for several days, and I had an expectation of and an investment in how I wanted things to be that morning. I felt rigid and stuck, and I momentarily wrestled with the urge to blame my client for the mental disturbance I was experiencing.

What followed over the next half hour was a series of emails in which we tried to sort the whole thing out — we figured out when we could reschedule (again) and tried to understand how our communication had got messed up. Should I have blamed her for her short-hand, BlackBerry writing style, which was just the kind of unclear and abrupt communication that was getting her into trouble with her staff? "No wonder you are having problems with your workers," I could have said. On the other hand, she could have blamed my inattention and noted that this was indicative of my chaotic thinking style and inability to make clear plans. Ultimately, we refrained from blaming each other, but we did note our modern technology dependency — why hadn't either of us just picked up the telephone to communicate?

Where should we place the blame? Well, that depends upon what we see as the problem. My client and I had clearly identified a faulty communication style between us, but she was no more responsible for my agitation that morning than I was for her emotions, whatever they were, when she discovered I wouldn't be meeting her at 10 AM. Before we blame, we can look inside ourselves to check our inner equilibrium: Is our mental health in balance? If we find that our mind is disturbed, we can either focus upon the disturbing emotions, our misperception of outer reality, or the misperception of our identity, the "I" in the equation.

If I had had more mental flexibility in that moment, then my mental health, my sense of peace and contentment, would not have been in jeopardy. But my sense of self, my "I" in that moment, was rigid; I certainly was physically capable of stopping what I was then doing and meeting with my client, but emotionally I could not. Further, I resented being put in the position of having to change unexpectedly. Who was this "I" who was in charge, who was *so controlling*? He's slippery and very difficult to find and seems to change moment to moment. He is malleable. He appears so solid when "I" am upset, but when my emotions ebb, he melts away. In an instant, he rises like a skyscraper, so solid and angry and righteous, but when "I" really look at him, and question whether he in fact is really there the way he appears, he becomes as ethereal as a rainbow we can never touch.

BLAME LEADS TO VIOLENCE, AWARENESS TO COMPASSION

The importance of informed awareness cannot be overstated. The road of ignorance and blame ultimately leads to violence, while wisdom leads to compassion. We've discussed this so far in purely personal terms, but it is not hard to see how it impacts larger communities and even nations. Naturally, violence is such an extreme manifestation of the disturbed emotions that it is, generally speaking, rare. In our everyday lives, we don't normally attack someone no matter how angry we are at them or how much we blame them.

But when violence and aggression do occur, it is invariably due to rigid concepts of self so fused with the disturbed emotions that the shift of awareness mind training calls for has become seemingly impossible to make.

Violence arises from anger, hatred, and a sense of separation from others. Typically, one is rigidly attached to a sense of self one sees as both inherently right and better than someone else's imagined persona, which is inherently wrong and "blamed" for one's own problems or the problems in the world. Further, this sense of self is supported by a strong adherence, or attachment, to the solidity and absoluteness of beliefs, values, and opinions. These beliefs are like the props of the rigid self. This "attachment" might take a literal form: I might defend what I own or possess, along with my right to own it, perhaps exclusively, from the claims of others. I am "the owner," and thus I am entitled to a piece of property, and you are a "threat," and I will fight you off or even kill you to keep from losing it. As it happens, sometimes the other person disagrees with our concepts: they believe they are the rightful "owner," and they claim we are the "threat," and so we fight for possession of the land or property and for the role or identity of "owner." Frequently, we might justify taking something from someone, or simply not sharing what we have, under the belief that I am more entitled to be happy than you. Your pain, your loss, and even your death are not my concern because my happiness, and that of those with whom I side, is more important than yours.

The only way to maintain such uncompassionate and uncaring points of view is with a concept of self that is fixed, immutable, and inherent. This is the very definition of selfishness. Indeed, even suicide is oftentimes merely this situation reversed: we can believe ourselves so inherently bad, so inherently in pain, and we are so rigidly fused with our false sense of self, that we see no hope for change or relief except to get rid of this troublesome self. However, even a little awareness that our identities are malleable, that our identities are concepts, can create separation from the concrete, problematic self and allow us take control of our own emotions and stem violence.

At its most extreme, this belief that my views and opinions are right, even flawless, while yours are of no value and, possibly, destructive is the basis for many wars, especially so-called religious wars. By fostering complete ignorance of the true nature of mind and total attachment to one's concepts, nations have justified killing "heretics" or those they define as opposed to one's faith or belief system. A wrong view that one race of people is superior over another race has been the motivator for many campaigns of genocide. Animal sacrifice is another example where violence upon another living being is justified from a wrong view. It is curious to Buddhists how one could kill another living being under the belief that it will cause happiness or good fortune, or even inspire blessings from a god or deity. It doesn't seem to correlate that the direct cause of happiness for one being can arise from the misery of another.

Sometimes, at this point, someone raises the issue of whether violence is ever "justified," such as to protect oneself or, in war, to kill fewer people in order to prevent wider bloodshed. In fact, the justification of "good intentions" is often what starts or perpetuates war and violence: we convince ourselves that our only motivation is protection or caring (which, conveniently enough, aligns with our sense of self as wholly good and righteous). But in my experience, such "justified violence" is nearly always motivated by hatred, dislike, self-righteousness, arrogance, and so on. So, while in theory there may be justified killing, it seems almost impossible to do so with the right mindset. I am suspicious that one can truly love one person, one country, one class of people, in juxtaposition to abhorring another. I think if one has a true love for the sacredness of life, and thus operates from a mind that is subdued and loving rather than angry or rageful, then there really is no such thing as justified killing or violence. Violence, whether internal or external, begets violence. Why? Because violence, in almost every case I can think of, is the result of a violent mind. It is next to impossible to have a violent act arise from love and concern for another's welfare.

Now, on a practical level we may need to act in self-defense. We may need to be assertive in protecting the lives of others. But I do not think these kinds of acts need to be generated by violence and aggression. They may be motivated by some level of attachment, but, unfortunately, we have to accept where we are at in our development. Among the Buddhist teachers I have studied with I have never heard the advice that one should be exploited or abused. Abuse and exploitation benefit no one. In mind training, we would seek to act in self-defense without a strong sense of anger or aggression toward another. Protecting another being is a compassionate act when motivated with the wish to benefit others absent of the wish to harm someone else. For example, we may wish to protect our parents from elder abuse, and we may need to be assertive, powerful, and dynamic to do so. But we come from the attitude of protecting our parents as opposed to seeking to merely hurt the abuser. Our actions might include reporting the abuser or initiating a punitive action, but we strive not to act with or be possessed by anger, vengeance, and so on. Our motivation is protection — of our parents, of other elders in the same facility (or future potential victims), and even perhaps of the abuser (from the self-harm of their hurtful actions). In general, an act of aggression toward another is the result of disturbed emotions, and yet acting with force, power, or assertiveness does not necessarily mean (or require) acting with aggression. It comes down to the motivation and the mindset.

This is, in essence, the reasoning behind the "nonviolent protest" of people like Gandhi and Martin Luther King. It is the understanding that concern for our own and others' well-being becomes something else if it results in violence. In addition, with discerning awareness, we learn not to "blame" another person for their violent actions: like the metaphor of the stick, we see that the violent person, when they strike, is under the control of their disturbing emotions. They suffer from ignorance of the true nature of reality, theirs and ours. They are suffering and in pain, and because of the misperceptions of the misleading mind, they have confused the source: they think it's outside of themselves, and have targeted us, when the cause is within. Thus, what happens if we strike them back? We only confirm their mistake by causing them more pain. If, however, we refuse to participate in their drama and respond with compassion and understanding, rather than with our own disturbed emotions, then hopefully we disrupt their "story" and create an opening for awareness.

This is the underlying ethics of mind training, for it helps us consider what kinds of actions lead to a more balanced and healthy mind and which actions create and perpetuate dis-ease within ourselves and others. It helps us remain flexible and accountable. It helps us understand the correct source of suffering and pain in any situation. It helps us distinguish between compassionately protecting others who are in need and vulnerable from the misleading ignorance that results in violence. To protect others, we may need to be strong, assertive, and even forceful. This is not the same as violence. Violence is driven by anger. Protection is driven by care. And the only effective way to reach and fix the source of violence is through wise compassion.

COMPASSION IN ACTION: LEARNING FROM MISTAKES

One of the hardest things to do when practicing mind training is to avoid getting caught up in self-blame and being too tough on ourselves. Our goal is to tackle every "problem," every disturbing emotion, and resolve and transform it through discerning awareness.

But as I've said, the path to the extinction of the disturbing emotions is long and winding. And so, we must pace ourselves, be kind to ourselves. This inner work is constant, and as it goes on, we need to stay in good cheer and not take ourselves and our journey too seriously. If we do, as we attempt to tackle bigger and bigger issues, we may find our energy flagging and feel discouraged. With discouragement, we can put ourselves down, put others down, and give up the process.

The work can be daunting even if the real cause of our problems is simple: our self-absorbed interest in our own agenda and happiness and our misunderstanding of what brings us contentment. In this terribly flawed formula, we believe, "If I get this and avoid that, I will be happy." And in fact, if we look deeply, we can see that every human-created problem in the world today — global warming, war, poverty, violent crime, the aggressive tension in our two-party political system, and so on — is the result of constantly overvaluing our own needs at the expense of others and confusing pleasures with lasting happiness. This situation represents a mind that is fundamentally agitated and dissatisfied.

There is no way for us to become mentally healthy without facing our errors, deficits, afflictions, and hang-ups. But we must do so with compassion, or else we may only cause more damage in the process. We must have courage, for as the adage goes, "No risk, no reward." And if we take risks, if we try, we are going to be wrong some of the time. We will make mistakes. Our disturbing emotions will always and inevitably arise. And that's okay. Indeed, it's to be expected. Lama Zopa Rinpoche embodied this attitude when a student of his, who is the principal of a secular school, once came to him in distress. It had been a particularly tumultuous year at her school, and at the end of the year, many of the parents withdrew their kids and a couple of teachers were let go. The student felt that she had failed as the school's principal, and she poured her heart out to Rinpoche, apologizing that she did not handle the situation in the best way possible. Rinpoche responded matter-of-factly, "Oh, it's okay. As long as we learn." The past is gone; why dwell? Our only job is to assess what, if anything, we could have done better, make a mental determination to do better next time, and let go of our disturbing emotions and move on without guilt.

This is easier said than done. We often need permission to allow ourselves to be compassionate toward ourselves, as I know firsthand. Once, when I was a student at the monastery in Nepal, I was given the rather impossible task of registering the monastery as a legal entity so that we would enjoy protection under Nepalese law. To navigate through the corrupt Nepalese bureaucracy, I hired a "lobbyist" to work on our behalf. On the day we were to receive official status, I presented a large sum of money to the lobbyist, who was to present it to the Minister of Education. The lobbyist absconded with the money — a severe blow. I dreaded telling this news to my mentor, the monastery's founder, Lama Yeshe, but when I did, I received a surprising life lesson. Lama looked off into the distance and calmly, matter-of-factly, said, "Well, you know you cannot trust Nepalese bureaucrats. Anyway, about the money, it's my students who make no mistakes that I really keep my eye on because I know they're not doing anything." And he walked away, never to bring up the topic again. Left to my own devices, I would have beat my "self" up for being so stupid and an idiot for losing the money. This would have fed the creation of a low self-image had I not been thwarted by Lama's shift in how to look at the situation without blaming "me." Just as surely, Lama Yeshe, with his level of awareness, free from the disturbing emotions, had only compassionate understanding arise in that very moment, and this helped me develop my own sense of compassion. Consequently I learned a life lesson I will never forget and from which I continue to grow.

To overcome our tendency to blame the wrong objects, we need to cultivate an ethic and philosophy of learning through mistake making. If we become "Learners" instead of "Mistake Avoiders," we can begin to tap into our vast inner potential. Living as a learner is a humble approach to life that amounts to a direct antidote to arrogance and pride. I have noticed, for myself, that I get most nervous in public speaking when I think I have to show up as the "expert." Almost by definition, an "expert" is so skilled as to be "perfect" in their field of expertise. To be less than perfect, to show areas or gaps in one's knowledge, is frowned on and the cause for embarrassment and the loss of "expert" status. Thus, to be an "expert" often requires the arrogant assumption that, in one's field at least, we have reached a sort of pinnacle of learning where it seems we have not much left to learn. When our egos become swollen with this belief, creative learning can easily come to a halt, and any mistake or error is seen as a threat. Thus, a danger in mind training is if we come to believe we have life all figured out.

To become our own therapist, our own coach, to truly come to grips with our unruly and unhealthy mind, we have to commit to being a lifelong student in that ever-fascinating topic of study, our own mind. Problems, challenges, disturbing events, and unsettling experiences are the best, fastest, and perhaps only way we can truly know ourselves and access the unfathomable inner qualities of our being. So give up the mirage of fixed identity — become a learner and transform your problems into happiness.

EXERCISE: CULTIVATING COMPASSION

We have become familiar with how our own mind creates problems for us. Hopefully, by now you are familiar with the disturbing emotions and harmful attitudes, feelings, and thoughts that arise and prevent you from being happy. In this exercise we look to expand this understanding to others. If you are feeling particularly affected by another person, and you feel particularly courageous, then use that person for this exercise.

First, get in touch with where your mind is at in this moment. In particular, if you are feeling pretty good or neutral, then provoke the mind a little to feel disturbed by bringing up some experience that may have been a bit upsetting. Now, as in earlier exercises, become acquainted with the disturbed emotion. Then, after just a few moments, direct your mental gaze to the world beyond you and look for all the people, even animals, that may be feeling just like you. Think also, if they don't feel like you at the present moment, they most likely have felt like you in the past and will feel like you in the future. Just like you move between depression, worry, happiness, and fear, they do too. Stay in this perception for some time. Now, if this is done really well, you will feel a sense of familiarity with their struggle. You will "see" that they are just like you, feel just like you, want to be happy just like you, and are disappointed just like you. When you get this feeling or insight, which is beyond an intellectual view, sit with it. Watch and feel the experience of that person or those people. Then slowly expand it to your community, your state, your country, your world. When we experience true empathy, we experience closeness and kinship with others. This is intimacy. At this point you will think and feel, "I wish they didn't have that problem." This sense of intimacy is, consequently, an extremely healthy mind.

Acknowledgments

When trying to acknowledge all the people who have contributed to the writing of this book, one begins to see the impossibility of that task. No knowledge is new, as it is said. This book, like all things, is a dependent arising of countless factors associated with countless beings. Where would I start to offer my acknowledgments? However, I will try to scale down my vision and express my gratitude to a few of the key people instrumental in bring these ideas to their present form.

It is truly unfeasible to even begin to express my gratefulness to my two spiritual mentors, Lama Thubten Yeshe and Lama Zopa Rinpoche. I am amazed they have stuck by me, since I feel I am one of the more difficult students they have had to contend with. It is not easy to convey that what I have learned from them had far less to do with the words they spoke than the embodiment of the ideas they have achieved. It is a perfect example of why we need role models if we really wish to actualize positive change and transformation. Just thinking of their tolerance and affection toward me brings tears to my eyes.

I would be remiss if I did not draw special attention to the unimaginable impact His Holiness the Dalai Lama has had upon me, personally and professionally. The ideas I have learned with respect to Buddhist thought have arisen because of his commitment to and diligence in sharing Buddhist thought with a nonsectarian and inclusive attitude with all people.

Just a step behind my two mentors and His Holiness is the unending support and confidence I receive from my wife of thirty-one years. We met and were married in Nepal, in the very monastery where I began my education in Buddhist psychology. I only pray that everyone's sense of aloneness can be alleviated with as amazing a partner and friend as I have found in Pam.

There are those Buddhist friends of mine who also offered clarity and advice on many fine points of Buddhist thought. My dear and longtime friend Jonathan Landaw deserves special recognition as well as Venerable Stephen Carlier. I wish to express my gratitude to Nicholas Ribush of the Lama Yeshe Wisdom Archive and my colleague Lorne Ladner, a psychologist and an author of Buddhist psychology.

Kendra Wilson was indispensable in working feverishly and offering endless support during the rough stages of the manuscript. Anyone who is writing a book needs a Kendra. Further, the team at New World Library, particularly Jason Gardner and Jeff Campbell, have been outstanding partners and, for some unknown reason, hung in there with me despite my picky and perfectionist tendencies. Louise Yates, my sister-in-law in Australia, also offered invaluable advice in helping me understand the PR and marketing principles in positioning the book in the marketplace.

My agent, Lorin Rees, has always been there to help me navigate this new world of writing and publishing. He has been a great supporter. When preparing the outline and proposal for the book, I found a gem of an editor in Seth Shulman. He deserves recognition not only for helping me formulate the organization of the book so that a publisher would even give it a glance but also for allowing his mind to be twisted like a pretzel in trying to understand my crazy ideas.

Further, it would be remiss of me to not send a special thank you to all my clients, not only those referred to in the book but to all those I have helped, and those for whom I was less than perfect. I feel particularly honored by my clients' courage and confidence that they could share the most vulnerable and intimate aspects of their life with someone who was, at first, a perfect stranger. I apologize to those whom I could not "save" and thank all of my clients for allowing me into their universe. What my clients may have never known is that I learned at least as much from our sessions as they did.

The rest of my family members, those in the United States and those in Australia, you have been unbelievable. I will never ask you again to share your opinions on another possible book cover, a passage from my childhood, or if I'm going to survive this writing torture — unless of course I, for some incomprehensible reason, decide to write another book.

Finally, I would like to thank Lyn and her entire team at the Sunrise Café. The bottomless coffee cup and wide booths live on and prove that with enough coffee and sweet smiles anyone can write a book.

About the Author

For over twenty years Karuna Cayton has worked as a psychotherapist, business psychologist, and coach to help people achieve a more balanced life. As founder of the Karuna Group (www.thekarunagroup.com), based in Soquel, California, he has dedicated his work to bringing the universal principles of Buddhist psychology to people in simple and clear terms so they can use these ideas in everyday life.

Karuna is a dedicated student of Lama Zopa Rinpoche, a Tibetan Buddhist master, and his late mentor, Lama Thubten Yeshe. Over thirty-five years ago, as a young undergraduate majoring in Asian Studies at Evergreen State College, he traveled to Nepal on the school's study abroad program where he became fascinated by the culture, in particular Tibetan Buddhism, and acquired a level of fluency in Nepali. After graduation, he returned to Nepal at the request of Lama Yeshe to teach English to the monks at Kopan Monastery and to create a Western Studies Program there. Karuna stayed for twelve years, until Lama Zopa Rinpoche one day advised Karuna to return to the US to study Western psychology and use his knowledge of Buddhist psychology to enhance the understanding of its principles within modern cultures.

After earning a master's in clinical psychology, Karuna worked at the Children's Health Council at Stanford University and was a member of the training program in Narrative Therapy at Mental Research Institute (MRI) in Palo Alto. In recent years Karuna's coaching clientele has included top executives from companies such as Aruba Networks, 3com, Martin Land Company, FPMT (a leading Buddhist organization), and Onstor. His work with Dominic Orr, CEO of Aruba Networks, was featured as the cover article for the November 2007 issue of *Fortune* magazine.

Karuna serves on the board of the Foundation for the Preservation of the Mahayana Tradition (FPMT, www.fpmt.org), a Buddhist organization with over 160 centers and projects around the world. He is also a trainer with the Potential Project, which brings mindfulness into corporate settings worldwide. He has taught classes at schools and corporations and has worked as a counselor and consultant with various public and private schools. He lives in Santa Cruz, California, with his wife and whichever of his three adult children needs a place to sleep. His website is www.thekarunagroup.com.

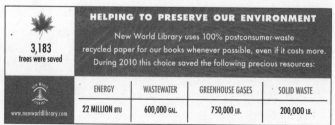